The Power Of Praying The Word of God

Unlocking God's Promises, Transform Your Life And See His Power Unleashed

Tom Flores

LIFE PUBLISHING HOUSE

The Power of Praying the Word
Copyright © 2026 by Tom Flores

All rights reserved. No part of this book may be reproduced, stored in a retrieval system, or transmitted in any form or by any means—electronic, mechanical, photocopying, recording, or otherwise—without prior written permission of the publisher, except for brief quotations used in reviews.

Scripture taken from the **New King James Version®**. Copyright © 1982 by Thomas Nelson. Used by permission. All rights reserved.

Published by
Life Publishing House

For information, contact:
Life Publishing House
www.lifepublishinghouse.com

Printed in the United States of America

Introduction

My wife Heather and I used to pray over our children often. We prayed sincere, heartfelt prayers. We believed God heard us. But if we are honest, we did not always see the kind of results we were hoping for. Things felt slow. At times, nothing seemed to change.

One day, Heather had a conversation with a friend. As they were talking, the topic of our adult children came up. She talked about how she had been praying for their lives, their family, and their careers. She said she kept asking God to bless them, to guide them, to help things move forward. Then she paused and admitted, "I'm praying... but I don't always feel like anything is really changing."

Her friend listened for a moment and then asked a question, "Have you ever tried praying God's Word over your children?" Heather thought about it. "Yeah... sometimes," she said. "I mean, I'll mention a verse here and there."

Her friend leaned in a little and said, "What if you made that the focus? What if you actually wrote your prayer out, added Scripture to it, and spoke the Word directly?"

Heather looked at her, curious. "I'm serious," her friend continued. "Write it down. Use the Word. And then pray that same prayer every single day. Don't just pray what you feel—pray what God has already said.""

So that is what we did. We wrote it out. We added the Word. And we began to speak those same Word-based prayers consistently. To our surprise, things began to shift. We started to see changes. The atmosphere began to shift in their lives. God began to move in a way we could see.

That experience changed how I view prayer. It is also why this book exists. Prayer is not just words we say. Prayer is how we come into agreement with God. When we pray the Word, we are speaking what God has already spoken, and His Word carries power. The Word of God is living and active, *"sharper than any two-edged sword"* (**Hebrews 4:12**).

The Word is truth, authority, and life. When we pray the Word, we take hold of what God has declared and bring it into our situation and stand on what heaven has already established. *"So shall My word be that goes forth from My mouth; it shall not return to Me void, but it shall accomplish what I please"* (**Isaiah 55:11**).

Praying the Word gives us access to His presence, His wisdom, and His power. *"Let us therefore come boldly to the throne of grace, that we may obtain mercy and find grace to help in time of need"* (**Hebrews 4:16**).

When we pray the Word, heaven responds. Angels respond to God's Word, *"Bless the Lord, you His angels, who excel in strength, who do His word"* (**Psalm 103:20**). They are *"ministering spirits sent forth to minister for those who will inherit salvation"* (**Hebrews 1:14**).

Praying is spiritual. It breaks the lies, tears down deception, and brings freedom. *"The weapons of our warfare are not carnal but mighty in God for pulling down strongholds"* (**2 Corinthians 10:4**).

The enemy is threatened by the Word because the Word exposes him. It brings light where there has been darkness. When Jesus was tempted, He answered every attack with, *"It is written"* (**Matthew 4:4, 7, 10**). He showed us how to stand—by speaking the Word.

This is what it means to pray the Word. It is not about finding the right words—it is about speaking the right truth. As the Word is spoken, faith rises, and confidence is established.

This book is built on that foundation. Each prayer is rooted in Scripture, designed to help you speak God's Word over your life, your family, your health, your mind, your future, and every situation you face. As you do, you are not just praying—you are aligning with God, declaring truth, and standing in what He has already said. The Word works when it is believed, spoken, and applied.

At this point, a question often comes up: Didn't Jesus say not to pray repetitive prayers?

"And when you pray, do not use vain repetitions as the heathen do. For they think that they will be heard for their many words" (**Matthew 6:7**).

Jesus was not correcting repetition—He was correcting empty repetition. The word "vain" means empty or without result. It describes prayers that are thoughtless or mechanical. Jesus was addressing people who believed that repeating words would force God to respond. Their prayers lacked faith and relationship.

Praying the Word is different. When you pray Scripture, you are not repeating words to be heard. You are speaking truth because you believe it. You are aligning your heart with what God has already said. The difference is not in the repetition. It is in the heart.

Vain repetition tries to produce results through words alone. Praying the Word rests in what God has already declared. The power in prayer does not come from saying more. It comes from truth and faith. *"The effective, fervent prayer of a righteous man avails much"* (**James 5:16**).

When you write out a prayer and speak it daily, you are not falling into empty repetition. You are building consistency. You are renewing your mind. You are speaking truth until it takes root in your heart.

This is not empty repetition. This is alignment.

How To Use This Book.

This book is meant to be used, not just read. The power is not in going through it once, but in praying the Word daily with intention, because **"the word of God is living and powerful, and sharper than any two-edged sword" (Hebrews 4:12).**

The prayers in this book are organized by life categories so you can easily find and pray over specific areas of need. You will find sections covering your daily walk with God, spiritual growth and freedom, healing and restoration, family and relationships, provision and finances, protection and peace, church and ministry, community and nation, salvation and evangelism, and special seasons of life. Whether you are praying for yourself, your family, your church, your finances, your health, or your nation, each prayer is designed to help you pray God's Word over that area consistently and effectively.

Take the prayers in this book and pray them every day until you begin to see breakthrough. Do not rush from one section to another looking for something new. Stay with the same Word-based prayer and let it take root, trusting that **"My word... shall not return to Me void, but it shall accomplish what I please" (Isaiah 55:11).**

Mark your place. Use bookmarks for the sections you plan to pray each day. Make it simple and easy to return to the same prayers consistently, because **"this Book of the Law shall not depart from your mouth, but you shall meditate in it day and night" (Joshua 1:8).**

Find a quiet place where you can focus. Remove distractions as much as possible. Even a few focused minutes are more powerful than scattered time, as Jesus said, **"when you pray, go into your room... and pray to your Father who is in the secret place" (Matthew 6:6).**

Read the prayers out loud. There is something significant about hearing the Word spoken. You are not only thinking it, you are declaring it. You are bringing your voice into agreement with what God has already said, because **"faith comes by hearing, and hearing by the word of God" (Romans 10:17).**

Commit to once a day, every day. Let it become part of your routine. Stay steady. Over time, you will begin to notice shifts in what you are praying the Word over, remembering to **"pray without ceasing" (1 Thessalonians 5:17).**

Stay with it until you see breakthrough, holding on to the promise: **"whatever things you ask when you pray, believe that you receive them, and you will have them"** (Mark 11:24).

Contents

PRAYERS FOR YOUR DAILY WALK WITH GOD

My Walk

Father, I walk worthy of the calling You have placed on my life. My steps are ordered by You, and my life is aligned with Your truth and purpose.

I follow You daily and walk in obedience to Your voice. I walk in the light, and my life remains open before You. Your Word guides me and gives direction to every step I take.

I abide in You, and my life produces lasting fruit. I walk by faith and remain steady and grounded in what You have spoken over my life.

I am led by Your Spirit. My path is directed by You, and my life reflects Your love and truth each day. You strengthen me within and establish me firmly through every season. I remain faithful to the calling You have given me. I continue walking forward with endurance, consistency, and confidence, knowing You are completing the work You began in me.

In Jesus name, Amen.

Scripture References: Ephesians 4:1, Luke 9:23, 1 John 1:7, Psalm 119:105, John 15:5, 2 Corinthians 5:7, Romans 8:14, Ephesians 5:2, Ephesians 3:16, 2 Timothy 4:7

Seeking God

Father, today I seek You with all my heart. I follow Your ways with peace, trust, and obedience. Guide my steps and make my path clear according to Your purpose for my life.

When I seek You, I find You. You are near to me, strengthening me, leading me, and surrounding me with Your peace. My soul thirsts for You, and my heart is refreshed and satisfied in Your presence.

As I draw near to You, quiet my heart and give me wisdom, clarity, and direction for this day. Let my life remain steady and fixed on You as I pursue You consistently and wholeheartedly.

In Your presence there is fullness of joy, peace, strength, and rest. Everything I need is found in You, and my heart remains secure in Your love and faithfulness.

In Jesus name, Amen.

Scripture References: Jeremiah 29:13, Matthew 6:33, Psalm 63:1, James 4:8, Proverbs 8:17, 2 Chronicles 15:2, Psalm 27:8, Psalm 16:11

Draw Near To God

Father, my heart honors You, reverences You, and desires to walk closely with You in every area of my life.

As I grow nearer to You, wisdom, understanding, and discernment grow within me. Your truth guides my life, and my heart values what is pleasing to You.

My life turns away from pride, compromise, and anything that pulls me away from Your presence. My desires are shaped by Your Spirit, and my life reflects what is holy, pure, and right before You.

My heart remains humble and sensitive to Your voice. I remain responsive to Your correction and aware of Your presence in my life. I walk before You with sincerity, reverence, and obedience.

Draw me close to You and reveal Your wisdom and Your ways as I continue seeking You. Establish my steps in righteousness and let my life bring honor and glory to Your name.

In Jesus name, Amen.

Scripture References: Proverbs 9:10, Proverbs 8:13, Psalm 25:14, Proverbs 14:26-27, Ecclesiastes 12:13, Psalm 86:11, Proverbs 16:6, Isaiah 33:6, Philippians 2:12, Colossians 1:10

Reading My Bible

Father, thank You for Your Word. As I read the Bible, open my eyes to understand, my ears to hear, and my heart to receive all that You want to teach me.

Your Word is a lamp to my feet and a light to my path. Give me wisdom, insight, and revelation as I study. Let Your truth take deep root in my heart and shape the way I think, live, and respond.

Teach me by Your Spirit. Help me remember what I read, apply it to my life, and grow in faith, understanding, and spiritual maturity. Let Your Word become alive within me.

Thank You that as I spend time in Scripture, I grow closer to You. My mind is renewed, my faith is strengthened, and my life is transformed by the power of Your Word.

In Jesus name, Amen.

Scripture References: Psalm 119:105, Psalm 119:18, Joshua 1:8, 2 Timothy 3:16-17, James 1:22, Romans 12:2, John 16:13, Colossians 3:16, Hebrews 4:12, Psalm 1:2-3

My Words

Father, I bring my words before You today. Let my speech reflect Your wisdom, Your truth, and Your heart in every conversation. May my words honor You and bring life to those around me.

Fill my speech with wisdom and understanding. Let my conversations be thoughtful, sincere, and guided by Your Spirit. Teach me to listen well and respond with grace and discernment.

My words bring encouragement, strength, and peace. What I speak reflects truth, builds others up, and strengthens the relationships You have placed in my life.

My tongue is guided by wisdom, and my responses are calm and steady. Patience, self-control, and understanding shape the way I communicate each day.

The words of my mouth and the meditation of my heart are pleasing in Your sight. My speech reflects faith, hope, truth, and life, and brings glory to Your name.

In Jesus name, Amen.

Scripture References: Psalm 141:3, Proverbs 18:21, Colossians 4:6, James 1:19, Proverbs 12:18, Ephesians 4:29, Proverbs 10:31, Psalm 19:14, Proverbs 15:1, Proverbs 16:23

God's Love

Father, I am loved by You. Your love surrounds me and nothing can separate me from Your love. I rest securely in the peace, strength, and confidence that comes from knowing You are with me.

Your love fills my heart, renews my mind, and strengthens me within. I am rooted and grounded in Your love, and through it You bring healing, stability, and wholeness into my life.

I thank You that I am Your child, fully known, fully accepted, and deeply loved by You. Perfect love drives out fear and fills my heart with peace and assurance.

I walk in love each day. Let the love You have shown me flow through my words, my actions, and the way I care for others. Your love never fails, and it faithfully carries me through every season of life.

In Jesus name, Amen.

Scripture References: Jeremiah 31:3, Romans 8:38-39, Romans 5:5, Ephesians 3:17-18, 1 Corinthians 13:4-7, 1 John 3:1, 1 John 4:18-19, Ephesians 5:2, 1 Corinthians 13:8

Prayer For Faith

Father, my faith grows stronger as I spend time in Your Word. Your truth settles deeply into my heart and shapes the way I think, speak, and live.

I walk by faith and remain confident in Your promises. My heart stays focused on Your truth and Your faithfulness in every season of life.

I trust You completely. What You have spoken, You are able to fulfill, and nothing is impossible for You. My confidence remains anchored in Your power, Your goodness, and Your perfect timing.

When I pray, I come before You with faith and expectation. I know You hear me, and I receive Your wisdom, direction, peace, and strength as I seek You.

My faith is active and alive in the way I follow You each day. I remain steady, fruitful, and firmly established in hope. Your promises remain true, and You are faithful in all that You say and do.

In Jesus name, Amen.

Scripture References: Romans 10:17, 2 Corinthians 5:7, Romans 4:3, Luke 1:37, Romans 4:21, James 1:6, Galatians 5:6, 1 Corinthians 16:13, Hebrews 10:23, 1 John 5:4

Trusting God

Father, thank You that Your way is perfect and that Your Word is faithful in every season of life. You are my Rock, my Fortress, my Deliverer, and my refuge. My trust is firmly established in You.

I place my future, my family, my calling, and every area of my life into Your hands. You are trustworthy in all Your ways, and Your wisdom directs me with clarity, peace, and understanding.

As I keep my eyes fixed on You, peace fills my heart and strength rises within me. Your presence steadies me, Your Word strengthens me, and Your faithfulness sustains me through every season.

I trust in You with all my heart. My hope is in You, my confidence is in You, and my life is secure in Your hands. You are my stronghold, my refuge, and my safe place, and my trust remains firmly established in You alone.

In Jesus name, Amen.

Scripture References: 2 Samuel 22:31-33, Psalm 2:12, Psalm 18:2-3, Psalm 20:7, Psalm 31:14-15, Psalm 56:3-4, Psalm 62:8, Proverbs 3:5-8, Proverbs 29:25, Isaiah 30:15, Nahum 1:7, 1 Timothy 4:10, Hebrews 2:13

Victory in Christ

Father, I stand in the victory You have given me through Christ. Thank You that You lead me in triumph and strengthen me with peace, confidence, and assurance.

I overcome by the blood of the Lamb and by the word of my testimony. In all things, I am more than a conqueror through Your love, and Your hand continues guiding and sustaining my life each day.

Your protection surrounds me, and Your favor rests upon me. Greater is He who is in me than he who is in the world. Fill me with wisdom, courage, endurance, and strength through the power of Your Holy Spirit.

I am strong in the Lord and in the power of His might. Every battle is under Your authority, and Your victory is already won. Today, I move forward with faith, peace, and expectation, knowing You go before me.

In Jesus name, Amen.

Scripture References: 2 Corinthians 2:14, Revelation 12:11, Romans 8:37, Isaiah 54:17, 1 John 4:4, Ephesians 6:10, 1 Samuel 17:47

Wisdom and Discernment

Father, thank You for giving me wisdom, understanding, and clarity. As I seek You, wisdom grows within me, and my life is guided by Your truth and Your Spirit.

You direct my steps and establish my path. My decisions are guided by Your wisdom, and my heart remains steady and confident as I trust in You.

Your Word is a lamp to my feet and a light to my path. It guides my life, shapes my thinking, and gives me direction for every season.

My heart remains humble, teachable, and attentive to Your voice. I walk with wisdom, make sound decisions, and recognize the opportunities You place before me.

I trust in You with all my heart. You direct my path, establish my steps, and lead me with wisdom, clarity, and purpose.

In Jesus name, Amen.

Scripture References: James 1:5, Proverbs 2:10-11, Psalm 37:23, Ephesians 1:17-18, Psalm 119:105, Philippians 1:9-10, Proverbs 9:10, Proverbs 3:5-6, Ephesians 5:15-16

Humility

Father, I humble myself before You and acknowledge that You are God and I am not. Everything I have, everything I am, and everything I accomplish comes from Your hand. My life belongs to You.

Give me a humble heart that remains dependent upon You. Let me walk closely with You, seek Your wisdom, and trust Your ways above my own understanding.

Keep my heart teachable and responsive to Your voice. Let me receive correction with gratitude, instruction with willingness, and truth with sincerity. Shape my character and continue Your work within me.

Protect me from pride, self-reliance, and a spirit that seeks its own way. Let humility, honor, and reverence for You be established deeply within my life.

Help me value others, serve others, and walk in love toward others. Let my life reflect the humility of Christ and the attitude of a servant's heart.

In Jesus name, Amen.

Scripture References: 1 Peter 5:6, James 4:6, Proverbs 3:5-6, James 1:21, Proverbs 11:2, Proverbs 9:9, Luke 14:11, Micah 6:8, Psalm 25:9, Philippians 2:3-8

24

Patience

Father, thank You for the work You are doing within me. As I walk with You each day, patience is growing stronger in my heart.

As I wait on You, my strength is continually renewed. My confidence remains anchored in Your faithfulness and in Your perfect timing.

Let patience have its perfect work in me. Produce endurance, wisdom, maturity, and spiritual strength within my life. Shape my character through every season and establish me firmly in truth and faithfulness.

I walk in love, kindness, and understanding. The peace of Christ guides my heart, and Your Spirit strengthens me to respond with wisdom and grace in every situation.

Thank You for producing endurance, peace, and maturity within me. I remain rooted in You, strengthened by Your presence, and confident that what You have begun in my life, You will faithfully complete.

In Jesus name, Amen.

Scripture References: James 1:4, Isaiah 40:31, Proverbs 14:29, James 1:2-4, Hebrews 10:36, Galatians 6:9, Ecclesiastes 3:11, 1 Corinthians 13:4, Colossians 1:11

Forgiveness

Father, thank You for the forgiveness and mercy. Because I have been forgiven, I choose to forgive others freely and sincerely from my heart. I release every offense, every hurt, and every wrong into Your hands.

I let go of bitterness and resentment, and I embrace the peace and freedom that come from walking in forgiveness. My life reflects mercy, compassion, grace, and love. I respond to others with the same kindness and patience that You continually show to me. Your love is shaping my heart and guiding my relationships.

I trust You with every situation and every injustice. My heart remains free, my mind remains at peace, and Your wisdom directs my responses. I walk forward in freedom, healing, and emotional strength.

Thank You that Your love continues working deeply within me. My heart is healed, my spirit is free, and my life is filled with peace as I continue walking in forgiveness and love.

In Jesus name, Amen.

Scripture References: Matthew 6:14-15, Colossians 3:13, Ephesians 4:31-32, Matthew 18:35, 1 Peter 4:8, Romans 12:17-19, Psalm 147:3, Luke 6:36, Proverbs 19:11

Strength to Endure Trials

Father, thank You for strengthening me in every season of life. Your power is at work within me, and my heart remains steadfast as I walk through every challenge and trial.

I remain faithful, consistent, and firmly established in You. Each season is producing maturity, wisdom, and deeper trust in Your faithfulness.

You renew my strength day by day. I continue moving forward with confidence, knowing that You are sustaining me, upholding me, and guiding my steps. Your grace is sufficient for me, and Your strength is continually at work in my life.

My eyes stay fixed on You, and the work You are doing in me is producing lasting fruit and eternal value.

In Jesus name, Amen.

Scripture References: Ephesians 3:16, James 1:2-4, Hebrews 12:1, Isaiah 40:31, Philippians 4:13, 2 Corinthians 12:9, Psalm 37:23-24, 1 Corinthians 15:58, 2 Corinthians 4:17

Self-Control

Father, thank You for the Holy Spirit who lives within me and strengthens me each day. You have given me power, love, and a sound mind.

I have self-control. My thoughts, emotions, words, and actions are governed by Your Spirit. Wisdom guides my decisions, and discipline is established in my life.

My mind is steady and fixed upon You. I am not moved by outward circumstances, changing situations, or passing emotions. My peace is found in You, and my confidence remains anchored in Your faithfulness.

I walk by the Spirit and live according to Your truth. My desires, habits, and choices are aligned with Your will. I remain focused, disciplined, and faithful in every season.

Thank You for strengthening me each day. I walk in self-control, wisdom, peace, and spiritual maturity as Your Spirit continues working within me.

In Jesus name, Amen.

Scripture References: Galatians 5:22-23, 2 Timothy 1:7, Isaiah 26:3, Galatians 5:16, Proverbs 16:32, Romans 13:14, 2 Peter 1:5-6, Philippians 4:7, 1 Corinthians 9:27

Integrity

Father, I desire to walk in integrity, honesty, and righteousness in every area of my life. My heart is established in Your truth, and my life reflects what is right and pleasing in Your sight.

Integrity guides my decisions, honesty shapes my words, and wisdom directs my steps. My character remains consistent in public and in private.

Help me to honor my commitments, speak truth, and live with a clear conscience before You. My choices reflect righteousness, discernment, and spiritual maturity as I walk according to Your Word.

My thoughts, attitudes, and actions are aligned with Your truth. I pursue what is honorable, excellent, and lasting. Love flows from a pure heart, a clear conscience, and sincere faith.

Thank You for producing integrity, wisdom, and righteousness within me.

In Jesus name, Amen.

Scripture References: Psalm 15:4, Psalm 25:21, Psalm 26:1-5, Proverbs 11:2-3, Matthew 5:41, Acts 23:1, Acts 24:16, Romans 9:1, 1 Corinthians 12:31, Philippians 1:10-11, 1 Timothy 1:5, 1 Timothy 1:19, 2 Peter 1:3

Overcoming Sin

Father, I thank You that through Jesus Christ, sin no longer has dominion over my life. Your Spirit strengthens me to walk in obedience, purity, and freedom.

I submit myself fully to You today. I resist the devil, and he flees from me. Every temptation loses its power through the authority of Jesus Christ.

I take every thought captive and bring it into obedience to Christ. Your grace empowers me to continue walking in righteousness and spiritual maturity. My life is being shaped by Your truth and established in Your presence.

Create in me a clean heart and renew a steadfast spirit within me. Let my life reflect the character of Christ in the way I think, speak, live, and respond each day.

Thank You for the victory, freedom, and new life found in Jesus Christ. I walk forward in faith, purity, obedience, and the strength of the Holy Spirit.

In Jesus name, Amen.

Scripture References: Romans 6:14, James 4:7, Galatians 5:16, 1 Corinthians 10:13, Psalm 51:10, Romans 12:2, 2 Corinthians 10:5, Ephesians 6:10-17, Philippians 4:8, Titus 2:11-12

Time and Priorities

Father, thank You that my life is ordered by You and that every day is held securely in Your hands.

Teach me to use my time wisely and to live each day with purpose. Let my focus remain on what matters most, and let my priorities align with Your will and Your calling for my life.

You order my steps and establish my path. My decisions are guided by Your wisdom, my mind is filled with clarity, and my life moves forward with direction and purpose. I seek first Your kingdom and place You at the center of my life. My time, energy, and attention are invested in what is valuable, meaningful, and lasting. My life reflects wisdom, discipline, and faithfulness.

Thank You for bringing order, focus, and clarity into every area of my life. I make the most of the opportunities You place before me, and I walk each day with purpose, intention, and spiritual maturity.

In Jesus name, Amen.

Scripture References: Psalm 90:12, Ephesians 5:15-16, Psalm 37:23, Matthew 6:33, Colossians 3:2, Romans 12:2, 1 Corinthians 14:40

Being led by the Holy Spirit

Father, I come before You now. Fill me with Your Holy Spirit today.

Refresh my heart, renew my mind, strengthen my spirit, and let Your peace and life flow deeply through every part of who I am.

Guide my thoughts, my words, my decisions, and my actions. Help me walk with wisdom and discernment in every situation. Let my life reflect Your presence and Your work within me.

Stir up every gift and calling You have placed inside of me. Use my life for Your glory and continue shaping me into who You have called me to be.

Give me strength to obey You, courage to trust You, and a heart that continually seeks after You.

In Jesus name, Amen.

Scripture References: Luke 11:13, Ephesians 5:18, Romans 15:13, Galatians 5:22-23, 2 Timothy 1:6, Acts 1:8, John 16:13, Ezekiel 36:27

Guidance in Decisions

Father, I bring every decision before You. I trust You with all my heart and lean on Your wisdom rather than my own understanding. Guide my steps and direct my path according to Your will.

Give me wisdom, discernment, and clarity. Let Your Word light my path and help me recognize the right direction. Remove confusion and fill my mind with understanding and peace.

Your voice leads me, and Your peace guides me. What is right becomes clear, and what is not from You fades away. My steps are ordered, established, and secure in Your hands.

Thank You for leading me faithfully. I walk forward with confidence, knowing that You are directing my life and giving me wisdom for every decision I face.

In Jesus' name, Amen.

Scripture References: Proverbs 3:5-6, Psalm 119:105, Psalm 32:8, James 1:5, Colossians 3:15, Isaiah 30:21, Psalm 37:23, Proverbs 16:9, 1 Corinthians 14:33

42

Gratitude and Contentment

Father, I thank You for Your goodness, Your faithfulness, and Your constant presence in my life. Every good thing I have comes from Your hand, and I choose to live with gratitude.

You are my Shepherd, and I do not lack. You have provided for me, sustained me, and carried me through every season. My heart is content because You are enough, and Your grace is sufficient for every need.

I will not live in anxiety, striving, or comparison. Peace fills my heart, and contentment settles my soul. I trust Your timing, Your provision, and Your plan for my life.

Thank You for Your many blessings. My life reflects gratitude, my heart overflows with praise, and I rejoice in Your goodness each day.

In Jesus' name, Amen.

Scripture References: 1 Thessalonians 5:18, Psalm 100:4, Philippians 4:11-12, Psalm 23:1, Hebrews 13:5, 1 Timothy 6:6, James 1:17, Philippians 4:6-7

44

Purpose and Calling

Father, I come before now, knowing that my life is in Your hands and that Your purpose for me is good. You guide my steps and lead me according to Your plan and timing. I trust You in every season of my life.

Thank you for wisdom, as I move forward today. Making clear what You are calling me to do, and I walk faithfully in it.

Thank You for the gifts and calling You have placed within me. Open the right doors for me, and bring the right opportunities and people into my life according to Your purpose.

Nothing in my life is wasted. Every season has a purpose to strengthen me, grow me, and draw me closer to You. I remain faithful, steady, and willing to follow wherever You lead.

I trust You with my future and purpose.

In Jesus name, Amen.

Scripture References: Jeremiah 29:11, Ephesians 2:10, Romans 11:29, Habakkuk 2:2, Revelation 3:8, Psalm 37:23, Romans 8:28, Philippians 1:6

PRAYERS FOR SALVATION AND EVANGELISM

Boldness in Faith

Father, boldness rises within me through the power of Your Spirit. You have given me a spirit of power, love, and a sound mind. My heart remains steady, my thoughts remain clear, and my faith remains strong in every situation.

I stand firm in what You have spoken over my life. I am not shaken by opinions, circumstances, or opposition, because my confidence is rooted in You.

I come before You boldly, knowing I am loved, received, and strengthened by Your grace. You are my help and strength in every season of life.

I am not ashamed of the gospel of Jesus Christ, and my life reflects faith, courage, and obedience to You.

Your Spirit fills me with boldness to walk fully in my calling. I continue moving forward with faith and con-fidence, trusting that You are leading and strengthening me each day.

In Jesus name, Amen.

Scripture References: 2 Timothy 1:7, Proverbs 28:1, Hebrews 4:16, Acts 4:29, Romans 1:16, 1 Corinthians 16:13, Acts 4:31, Hebrews 10:39

Salvation For The Lost

Father, I lift up _________________ before You. Draw them by Your Holy Spirit and reveal Jesus Christ to them in a real and personal way. Open their eyes to see the truth and their heart to receive Your love.

Holy Spirit, convict their heart and draw them to salvation. Remove every veil, every deception, and every barrier that keeps them from fully knowing You.

Let the goodness of God lead them to repentance. Reveal Your mercy, grace, and forgiveness, and let faith rise within them as they hear and receive Your truth.

I declare that their heart turns toward You and that they will confess Jesus Christ as Lord. Let their life be transformed by Your love, filled with Your peace, and established in salvation.

In Jesus' name, Amen.

Scripture References: John 6:44, John 16:8, Romans 2:4, 2 Corinthians 4:4-6, Romans 10:9-10, Romans 10:17, Acts 16:31.

Sharing Jesus

Father, thank You for empowering me to be a witness for Jesus Christ. Fill me with boldness, wisdom, and compassion as I share Your truth with those around me.

Give me the right words at the right time. Let my speech be filled with grace and truth, and let every conversation be guided by Your Spirit. Open doors for me to share the hope that is found in Jesus.

Fill my heart with love for people. Let me see others the way You see them and respond with compassion, humility, and genuine care. May my life reflect the heart and character of Christ in every situation.

Let my life shine with Your light. May people see Jesus through my words, my actions, and the way I live. Use me to bring encouragement, hope, and truth wherever I go.

Holy Spirit, lead every conversation and every opportunity You place before me.

In Jesus name, Amen.

Scripture References: Luke 12:12, Colossians 4:6, 1 Corinthians 13:4, Philippians 2:5, Matthew 5:16, Colossians 4:5, Ephesians 4:29, Acts 1:8

Someone Angry with God

Father, I lift up _______________ to You today. You see every hurt, disappointment, question, and struggle hidden within their heart. Nothing is unseen by You, and nothing is beyond Your ability to heal, restore, and redeem.

Bring healing where there has been pain, peace where there has been turmoil, and hope where there has been discouragement. Let Your presence bring comfort, clarity, and rest to every wounded place.

Reveal Your love and faithfulness. Let them know they are seen, valued, loved, and never forgotten by You.

Draw them close to You and strengthen their faith. Restore what has been broken, renew trust in Your goodness, and let them experience the depth of Your grace, mercy, and unfailing love.

In Jesus' name, Amen.

Scripture References: Psalm 34:18, Matthew 11:28, Romans 2:4, Psalm 147:3, Isaiah 41:10, James 1:5, Luke 15:20, Romans 8:38-39, Lamentations 3:22-23, John 6:44

PRAYERS FOR SPIRITUAL GROWTH AND FREEDOM

Temptation

Father, I place every area of my life into Your hands. Thank You for Your faithfulness and for the strength You provide each day. You guide my steps, direct my path, and lead me in ways that honor You. You do not lead me into temptation, but You deliver me from evil and provide a way for me to stand firm.

Your Word is hidden in my heart and shapes the way I think and live. When temptation comes, I stand upon Your truth and declare, "It is written." Your Word gives me wisdom, strength, and victory.

Your Spirit is at work within me. I walk by the Spirit, and my desires are aligned with Your will. Your grace strengthens me to live in obedience, self-control, and spiritual maturity.

Thank You for strengthening me as I walk faithfully with You. I stand firm, endure with confidence, and overcome through the power of Your Word and the strength of Your Spirit.

In Jesus name, Amen.

Scripture References: 1 Corinthians 10:13, Matthew 6:13, Psalm 119:11, Galatians 5:16, Romans 6:14, James 4:7, Romans 13:14, James 1:12, Matthew 4:4, 7, 10

Social Media

Father, I place my mind, my attention, and my time into Your hands. Help me to use technology with wisdom and self-control. Let nothing distract me from Your presence, Your purpose, or the life You have called me to live.

My identity is found in You and not in likes, followers, opinions, or approval. My value comes from Your love, and my confidence is established in Your truth.

Thank You for helping me guard my thoughts and protect my peace. My mind is calm, focused, and disciplined. I choose what is life-giving, healthy, and pleasing to You.

I am free from distraction, comparison, and unhealthy dependence on social media. My attention is directed toward what matters most, and my heart remains sensitive to Your Spirit.

In Jesus name, Amen.

Scripture References: Romans 12:2, Philippians 4:8, Proverbs 4:23, Galatians 5:22-23, Colossians 3:2, Psalm 90:12, 1 Corinthians 6:12, Psalm 101:3, Hebrews 12:2, Isaiah 26:3

Protection From Deception

Father, I ask for spiritual discernment and understanding. Let the Holy Spirit lead me into all truth and guard me from every deception, lie, counterfeit, and false influence.

Expose every hidden scheme of the enemy. Bring darkness into the light and reveal anything that is not from You. Give me wisdom to recognize truth, reject error, and walk in Your ways. Your Word is a lamp to my feet and a light to my path.

I will not be led by fear, emotions, appearances, or human reasoning alone, but by Your Spirit and by the truth of Your Word. Thank You for giving me the mind of Christ. My life is established in truth, my steps are directed by wisdom, and every plan of deception against me, my family, and my calling is exposed and overcome by the light of Jesus Christ.

In Jesus name, Amen.

Scripture References: John 16:13, John 8:32, Ephesians 5:11, 2 Corinthians 2:11, James 1:5, Psalm 119:105, Hebrews 5:14, 1 Thessalonians 5:21, Ephesians 1:17-18, 1 Corinthians 2:16.

Generational Bondages

Father, thank You that through Jesus Christ, freedom is established in my life. Every chain is broken. Every stronghold is torn down. Every unhealthy pattern that has sought to influence my life and family is replaced with Your truth, Your freedom, and Your blessing.

The blood of Jesus covers my life, my family, and every generation connected to me. Freedom, healing, restoration, peace, and blessing flow through my family line. My household belongs to the Lord. I declare that future generations will know You, serve You, and walk in Your ways.

Your hand is upon my children, my grandchildren, and those who come after me. In the name of Jesus, every assignment of the enemy against my life and family is broken. Strongholds are torn down, truth is established, and every strategy of the enemy is exposed and defeated by the power of God.

In Jesus name, Amen.

Scripture References: John 8:36, 2 Corinthians 5:17, 2 Corinthians 10:4-5, Colossians 1:13, Galatians 3:13, Romans 12:2, Joshua 24:15, Isaiah 54:17, Joel 2:25, Acts 16:31

Prayer Over My Mind

Father, thank You that You have given me a sound mind through Jesus Christ. My thoughts are steady, clear, and aligned with Your truth. Your presence brings peace and stability to my heart and mind.

Your Word renews my mind and shapes the way I think and live. I set my mind on You, and my thoughts are guided by Your wisdom and truth.

Your peace guards my heart and mind. I walk with clarity, discernment, and understanding as You direct my decisions and establish my steps.

Wisdom and understanding increase within me. I recognize truth, make sound decisions, and walk confidently in the direction You are leading me. My mind remains focused, disciplined, and attentive to Your voice.

The mind of Christ is at work within me. I think according to Your truth, walk in Your wisdom, and live according to Your purpose for my life.

In Jesus name, Amen.

Scripture References: 2 Timothy 1:7, Romans 12:2, 2 Corinthians 10:5, Colossians 3:2, Philippians 4:7-8, 1 Corinthians 2:16, Isaiah 26:3, James 1:5

Future

Father, I place my future completely into Your hands. You know the plans you have for me. My life is secure in You, and Your hand remains upon me through every season.

You go before me and prepare the way ahead. You direct my steps, establish my path, and guide me with wisdom and clarity. My future is being shaped by Your purpose and Your faithfulness.

I trust You with every step that lies ahead and rest in the confidence that You are guiding my life.

You are working in my life. What You have begun in me, You will faithfully complete.

My future is filled with hope because my future is in You. I walk forward with confidence, peace, and expectation, knowing that You are leading me into all that You have prepared for me.

In Jesus name, Amen.

Scripture References: Jeremiah 29:11, Psalm 31:15, Isaiah 45:2, Proverbs 3:5-6, Isaiah 41:10, Romans 8:28, Revelation 21:5, Philippians 1:6

Loneliness

Father, thank You for being constantly present in my life. Your presence surrounds me, strengthens me, and brings peace to my heart. I rest in the assurance that You are near to me and faithfully caring for every part of my life.

Your love restores me, encourages me, and reminds me that I am never alone.

Lead the right people into my life. Surround me with healthy relationships, faithful friendships, and meaningful connections that bring wisdom, encouragement, support, and genuine fellowship.

I am loved, seen, valued, and cared for by God. His presence is with me, His peace fills me, and His joy strengthens me each day.

My life is filled with purpose, fellowship, and the goodness of God.

In Jesus name, Amen.

Scripture References: Hebrews 13:5, Psalm 34:18, Psalm 68:6, John 14:27, Psalm 46:1, 1 John 4:18, Psalm 139:1-2, Romans 15:13, Proverbs 17:17, Psalm 16:11

Letting Go of Offense

Father, today I release every offense, hurt, disappointment, and painful word into Your hands. I choose forgiveness, freedom, and peace. I will not allow offense to take root in my heart or influence my life.

In the name of Jesus, I break agreement with every spirit of offense, bitterness, resentment, and unforgiveness. My thoughts, emotions, and responses are governed by Your Spirit and established in Your truth.

I forgive those who have hurt, rejected, misunderstood, criticized, or wronged me. I release them into Your hands and trust You with every situation. Your peace fills my heart, and Your grace gives me strength to walk in love.

The enemy gains no advantage in my life through offense. My heart remains clean, my spirit remains free, and my focus remains on You. I walk forward in healing, freedom, peace, and wholeness through Jesus Christ.

In Jesus' name, Amen.

Scripture References: Colossians 3:13, Ephesians 4:31-32, Proverbs 4:23, 1 Peter 4:8, Hebrews 12:15, Luke 17:1, James 1:19-20, 2 Corinthians 2:10-11, Colossians 3:15, Romans 12:18

Being Unoffendable

Father, today I choose to walk above offense. My peace is not controlled by the words, actions, opinions, or attitudes of others. My heart remains anchored in You and established in Your truth.

I release every hurt, disappointment, misunderstanding, and irritation into Your hands. Love fills my heart, grace shapes my responses, and wisdom guides my words. I refuse to allow offense to take root within me.

The peace of God rules my heart. Patience, humility, mercy, and self-control are growing within me through the work of the Holy Spirit. My spirit remains calm, steady, and free.

Thank You for helping me walk in love and maturity. My heart stays tender, my mind stays at peace, and my life remains firmly established in Your presence. I am free from offense and full of the peace of God.

In Jesus' name, Amen.

Scripture References: Colossians 3:13, Ephesians 4:31-32, Proverbs 19:11, James 1:19-20, Colossians 3:15, 1 Peter 4:8, Romans 12:18, Galatians 5:22-23

Guarding the Heart Against Bitterness

Father, guard my heart and keep it free from bitterness. Let no hurt, disappointment, offense, or painful experience take root within me. Fill my heart with Your peace, Your love, and Your grace.

I choose to forgive quickly and release every offense into Your hands. I will not allow resentment, anger, or bitterness to grow within me. My heart remains soft, tender, and responsive to Your Spirit.

Thank You for healing every wounded place and restoring my soul. Your peace rules in my heart, Your love fills my life, and Your truth guides my thoughts and responses.

I guard my heart carefully and keep my focus on You. Bitterness has no place in my life. My heart is established in forgiveness, love, peace, and freedom through Jesus Christ.

In Jesus' name, Amen.

Scripture References: Proverbs 4:23, Ephesians 4:31-32, Colossians 3:13, Hebrews 12:15, 1 Peter 4:8, Philippians 4:7, 2 Corinthians 2:10-11, Romans 12:21, Romans 12:18, Psalm 147:3

Gluttony and Overindulgence

Father, give me strength to walk in self-control, discipline, and wisdom. My body, mind, desires, and choices belong to You. Let my life honor You in the way I live each day.

Through the power of the Holy Spirit, I overcome unhealthy habits, overindulgence, and every appetite that seeks to control me. I am led by Your Spirit, not by my flesh. I walk in freedom, balance, and moderation.

Renew my mind through Your Word and strengthen my will. Give me wisdom in my eating, spending, emotions, and daily decisions. Let discipline, consistency, and healthy habits become established in my life.

My body is the temple of the Holy Spirit. I choose what is beneficial, life-giving, and honoring to You. Through Jesus Christ, I walk in self-control, victory, and lasting freedom.

In Jesus' name, Amen.

Scripture References: Galatians 5:22-23, 1 Corinthians 6:19-20, Romans 13:14, Titus 2:11-12, Romans 12:2, Proverbs 25:28, John 8:36, 1 Corinthians 10:31.

Favor

Father, thank You for Your favor upon my life. Just as You gave Joseph favor wherever he went, let Your favor rest upon me and be evident in all that I do.

I find favor in Your sight and in the eyes of those around me. Favor rests upon me with employers, leaders, coworkers, clients, and those You place in my path. Let wisdom, excellence, and integrity mark my life.

Open doors of opportunity before me. Connect me with the right people, position me in the right places, and bring increase, promotion, and provision according to Your will.

Your favor surrounds me like a shield. Your hand is upon me, Your goodness goes before me, and Your blessing follows me wherever I go.

In Jesus name, Amen.

Scripture References: Genesis 39:2-4, 21-23, Psalm 5:12, Proverbs 3:4, Deuteronomy 28:12-13, Psalm 90:17, Luke 2:52, Revelation 3:8

PRAYERS FOR FAMILY AND RELATIONSHIPS

My Home

Father, thank You for my home and for Your hand of blessing upon it. I dedicate this house to You and invite Your presence to fill every room with peace, joy, and love.

Your protection rests over this home. You watch over my family, guard what You have entrusted to me, and surround this house with Your favor and care.

Peace fills this home. Love grows here. Wisdom guides every decision, and kindness shapes every relationship. Let this be a place of rest, encouragement, and spiritual strength.

Thank You for providing for this household. Every need is supplied, every responsibility is met, and Your faithfulness remains constant in every season.

Your blessing rests upon this home. Goodness, mercy, peace, provision, and protection remain here, and this house honors You in all that it does.

In Jesus' name, Amen.

Scripture References: Joshua 24:15, Psalm 91:1-2, Psalm 127:1, Proverbs 24:3-4, Psalm 23:6, Philippians 4:19

Protection Over Family

Father, my family is covered by You. You are our refuge and our fortress, and we dwell secure under Your protection. No evil comes near us, and no harm overtakes us. We are kept and preserved in every place we go.

Your angels surround us and guard us in all our ways. We are watched over, protected, and kept. You watch over our coming in and our going out. Every step is covered, and every path is secure.

The Lord is our keeper. You are our shade, and You preserve our lives. You are a shield around us. We are defended, covered, and sustained by You.

Our home is established in peace. There is safety, rest, and stability within it. You command protection over everything that belongs to us. What is entrusted to us is preserved. We dwell in Your presence, and we remain secure in Your care.

In Jesus' name, Amen.

Scripture References: Psalm 91:1-2, Psalm 91:10-11, Psalm 121:7-8, Psalm 121:5, Psalm 3:3, Job 1:10, Proverbs 18:10, Psalm 46:1, Psalm 91:1

Marriage

Father, thank You for my marriage and for the spouse You have given me. Protect my spouse physically, emotionally, mentally, and spiritually. Guard their heart, mind, and life. Surround them with Your favor, wisdom, strength, and peace wherever they go.

Let love, honor, faithfulness, and trust continue growing between us. Keep our hearts devoted to You and devoted to one another. Lead us away from temptation and protect our marriage from anything that would seek to weaken, divide, or harm it.

Let purity, integrity, and faithfulness mark our lives and our relationship. Peace rules in our home, and grace flows between us. We are quick to forgive, quick to encourage, and quick to build one another up.

Thank You for watching over our marriage. Your hand is upon us, Your presence fills our home, and our relationship continues to grow stronger through Your love and grace.

In Jesus' name, Amen.

Scripture References: Genesis 2:24, 1 Corinthians 13:4-8, Ephesians 5:25, Colossians 3:13-15, James 1:19, Matthew 6:13, Ecclesiastes 4:9-10, Hebrews 13:4, 1 Thessalonians 5:11, Psalm 127:1

Prayer For My Husband

Father, I lift my husband before You today. Thank You for the man You created him to be. Strengthen him in every area of his life and establish him in Your wisdom, peace, and purpose. Let his steps be ordered by You and his heart remain steadfast in faith.

Protect him physically, emotionally, mentally, and spiritually. Guard his heart and mind, and keep him from temptation, distraction, and every scheme of the enemy. Let Your hand remain upon him wherever he goes.

Bless the work of his hands and establish all that he does. Give him wisdom in every decision, favor in every opportunity, and success in the assignment. Let provision, fruitfulness, and strength increase in his life.

Fill him with courage, peace, and confidence. May he become everything You have called him to be and walk fully in the purpose You have prepared for him.

In Jesus' name, Amen.

Scripture References: Psalm 1:3, Proverbs 2:6, Proverbs 3:5-6, Ephesians 5:25, Joshua 1:9, Isaiah 26:3, Psalm 90:17, Psalm 5:12, Matthew 6:13, 1 Corinthians 16:14

Prayer For My Wife

Father, I lift this woman to You today. Thank You that she is loved, chosen, valued, and secure in You. Her identity is found in Christ, and her worth is established by Your love and truth.

In the name of Jesus, I come against every spirit of insecurity, jealousy, comparison, rejection, and fear that would seek to influence her heart or mind. Let every lie be replaced with truth. Fill her with confidence, peace, and a deep awareness of who she is in You.

Let her heart be secure, her mind be at peace, and her spirit be strengthened. May she walk in wisdom, grace, humility, and joy.

Your favor rests upon her life. Your peace guards her heart and mind, and Your love surrounds her daily. She is strong, secure, confident, and firmly established in Your purpose for her life.

In Jesus' name, Amen.

Scripture References: Psalm 139:14, Ephesians 1:4-6, Philippians 4:7, 2 Timothy 1:7, Proverbs 14:30, James 3:16, Colossians 3:15, 1 John 4:18, Isaiah 54:17, Romans 8:37-39

Family Unity

Father, let unity, peace, and love fill this family. Bind our hearts together in strength, understanding, and compassion. Let kindness, patience, forgiveness, and grace flow freely within our family.

In the name of Jesus, we come against division, strife, offense, misunderstanding, and every scheme of the enemy designed to bring separation into this family. Let every wall be torn down, every wound be healed, and every relationship be strengthened through Your love.

Peace rules in this home. Anger, bitterness, resentment, and offense have no place here. Harmony, respect, humility, and honor are established within our family.

Protect this family and strengthen every relationship. Draw each of us closer to You and closer to one another. Let Your presence fill our family with joy, stability, love, and unity.

In Jesus' name, Amen.

Scripture References: Psalm 133:1, Colossians 3:13-14, Ephesians 4:29, James 1:19, Colossians 3:15, Romans 12:10, John 17:21, Ephesians 6:11, Joshua 24:15, 2 Corinthians 2:10-11, Ephesians 4:31-32

My Children

Father, I place my children into Your hands. Thank You that they are loved by You, known by You, and held securely in Your care. Your hand is upon their lives, and Your purpose for them will be fulfilled.

Surround my children with Your protection wherever they go. Command Your angels concerning them to guard them in all their ways. Let angels encamp around them and keep them safe from danger, harm, accidents, and every evil thing.

Guide their steps and direct their path. Give them wisdom, discernment, and understanding in every decision. Let them walk in truth, integrity, and the purpose You have prepared for their lives.

Fill them with peace, strength, courage, and confidence. Let Your favor rest upon them and surround them everywhere they go. Thank You that my children are protected, guided, and blessed.

In Jesus' name, Amen.

Scripture References: Psalm 91:11-12, Psalm 34:7, Psalm 121:7-8, Isaiah 54:13, Proverbs 3:5-6, James 1:5, Numbers 6:24-26, Psalm 23:6, Hebrews 1:14, Jeremiah 29:11

Protection Over My Daughter

Father, I place _________________ into Your hands today. She dwells in Your presence and rests under Your protection. You are her refuge, her fortress, and her safe place.

Surround her with Your angels and guard her wherever she goes. Watch over her coming in and her going out. Let every step be ordered, protected, and secure.

No weapon formed against her will prosper. Your hand is upon her life, and Your covering surrounds he. Fill her heart with peace and confidence. Fear has no place in her life because she is securely held in Your care. Her mind is at rest, and her heart is steady in You.

Thank You for protecting, preserving, and watching over her. Your goodness surrounds her, Your presence goes before her, and Your peace remains with her every day.

In Jesus' name, Amen.

Scripture References: Psalm 91:1-2, Psalm 91:10-11, Psalm 121:7-8, Proverbs 18:10, Isaiah 54:17, Job 1:10, Isaiah 26:3, Psalm 34:7

Prayer for My Son

Father, I lift my son _________________ before You today. Thank You that he is known by You, loved by You, and called according to Your purpose. Your hand is upon his life, and his future is secure in You.

Give him wisdom, discernment, and courage. Let Your Word take deep root in his heart and guide every decision he makes. May he grow in character, strength, integrity, and favor with You and with others.

Surround him with Your protection. Command Your angels concerning him and guard him wherever he goes. Keep him from harm, deception, temptation, and wrong influences. Let no weapon formed against him prosper.

Thank You that Your blessing rests upon my son. May he know Your voice, walk in Your purpose, and experience Your favor all the days of his life. He is protected, guided, strengthened, and securely held in Your hands.

In Jesus' name, Amen.

Scripture References: Jeremiah 1:5, Joshua 1:9, Psalm 91:11, Isaiah 54:17, Psalm 119:11, Luke 2:52, Proverbs 13:20, 2 Timothy 1:7, Numbers 6:24-26

My Children in School

Father, I place my children into Your hands. Thank You that they are loved by You, protected by You, and guided by Your wisdom each day.

Your hand is upon them wherever they go. Keep them safe, guard their hearts and minds, and surround them with Your peace and favor. Let them grow in wisdom, understanding, confidence, and strength.

Favor rests upon them with teachers, friends, and those around them. Surround them with healthy influences and relationships that encourage them and help them grow. Give them courage to do what is right, wisdom in every decision, and success in their studies. Let them learn well, stay focused, and use the gifts You have placed within them.

Thank You for watching over my children. Your peace fills them, and Your blessing remains upon their lives.

In Jesus' name, Amen.

Scripture References: Isaiah 54:13, Psalm 121:7-8, James 1:5, Philippians 4:7, Proverbs 13:20, 2 Timothy 1:7, Luke 2:52, Psalm 91:11, Proverbs 22:6, Numbers 6:24-26

Prayer for a Teenage Child

Father, _______________ is known by You, formed by You, and called according to Your purpose. Their identity is established in You, and their confidence comes from who You say they are. Let them grow in wisdom, character, and favor with You and with others. Your Word is hidden in their heart and guides their choices. Their mind is being renewed by Your truth, and their life is being shaped by Your wisdom. Give them discernment, understanding, and clear direction for every season.

In the name of Jesus, protect them from every wrong influence, deception, temptation, and distraction. Surround them with wise friendships and healthy relationships that encourage their faith and strengthen their walk with You. Let them be strong, courageous, and unwavering in what is right. Lead them in the path You have prepared, and let them walk confidently in Your calling.

In Jesus' name, Amen.

Scripture References: Jeremiah 1:5, Psalm 119:11, Romans 12:2, Luke 2:52, Joshua 1:9, 1 Timothy 4:12, Proverbs 13:20, Ephesians 6:1-2, Isaiah 54:13, Ephesians 2:10

Prayer for an Adult Child

Father, I thank You for my child and for the purpose You have over their life. Guide their steps and give them wisdom in every decision they make. Keep their heart close to You and let them clearly recognize Your voice. Protect them wherever they go. Surround them with the right relationships, wise counsel, and people who will strengthen their faith and character.

Let peace fill their mind and heart, and remove fear, confusion, and anxiety. Provide for every need they have and open the right doors at the right time. Lead them in integrity, maturity, and truth. If they begin to drift, draw them back to You and remind them that they are loved, called, and never beyond Your reach.

Bless their future with favor, direction, and hope. Establish the work of their hands and let their life bring glory to You.

In Jesus' name, Amen.

Scripture References: Proverbs 3:5-6, James 1:5, John 10:27, Psalm 121:7-8, Proverbs 13:20, Philippians 4:7, Philippians 4:19, Proverbs 11:3, Luke 15:20, Jeremiah 29:11

Prayer for Grandchildren

Father, thank You for my grandchildren. They are a gift from You, and Your hand is upon their lives. May they grow in wisdom, understanding, and favor with You and with others as they walk in the purpose You have prepared for them.

Teach them Your ways, guide their choices, and establish them in truth. May they grow strong in character, faith, kindness, and courage.

Protect them wherever they go. Surround them with Your angels and keep them safe from harm, danger, deception, and wrong influences. Let great peace rest upon their hearts and minds.

Thank You that my grandchildren are blessed, protected, and loved by You. Their steps are ordered, their future is secure, and Your favor and goodness will follow them all the days of their lives.

In Jesus' name, Amen.

Scripture References: Psalm 127:3, Isaiah 54:13, Psalm 119:11, Luke 2:52, Psalm 121:7-8, Psalm 91:11, Proverbs 4:23, Joshua 1:9, Colossians 3:12, Ephesians 2:10

A Strong-Willed Child

Father, this child is a gift from You, entrusted with strength, energy, and purpose.

Give them a teachable heart and a willing spirit. Let wisdom take root early, and let their strength be directed toward what is good, right, and pleasing to You. May they grow in understanding, maturity, and self-control.

Turn determination into perseverance, courage, and leadership. Let their strong will help them overcome obstacles, stand firm in truth, and succeed in the purpose You have prepared for their life. May they learn to use their gifts with wisdom and humility.

Thank You that this child grows in wisdom, stature, and favor with God and with people. Their life is established in peace, character, and strength, and the qualities You have placed within them will prosper them and bring glory to You.

In Jesus' name, Amen.

Scripture References: Psalm 127:3, Proverbs 22:6, Proverbs 15:5, Proverbs 16:32, Galatians 5:22-23, Ephesians 6:1-2, Isaiah 54:13, Hebrews 12:11, Luke 2:52, Joshua 1:9, Proverbs 3:5-6

Revival in My Family

Father, let revival begin in my family. Draw every heart closer to You and awaken a deep hunger for Your presence, Your Word, and Your ways. Let salvation, faith, and spiritual life flourish throughout every generation.

Pour out Your Spirit upon my family. Let our home be filled with prayer, worship, peace, and the joy of the Lord. May each family member grow in their relationship with You and walk closely with Your Spirit.

Raise up mighty men of God and women of God from this family. Let our children, grandchildren, and future generations love You, serve You, and walk faithfully in the purpose You have prepared for their lives.

Let Your blessing, favor, and presence rest upon this family. May our lives bring glory to Jesus, and may generations after us continue to know You, follow You, and proclaim Your goodness.

In Jesus' name, Amen.

Scripture References: Joshua 24:15, Acts 2:17, Psalm 85:6, Joel 2:28, Isaiah 54:13, Psalm 115:14-15, Acts 16:31, Psalm 145:4, 2 Timothy 1:5, John 17:21

Success in Education

Father, I bring my education before You. Thank You for giving me wisdom, understanding, and the ability to learn. My mind is clear, focused, and ready to receive knowledge.

I have the mind of Christ. I understand, retain, and apply what I study with confidence. Insight increases, understanding grows, and what I learn produces fruit in my life.

Diligence and discipline are established in me. I stay focused, consistent, and productive. I do not grow weary, but continue forward with strength and endurance.

Thank You for favor, opportunity, and success. You guide my steps, open the right doors, and help me excel in all that You have called me to learn and accomplish.

In Jesus' name, Amen.

Scripture References: Psalm 32:8, James 1:5, Proverbs 2:6, 1 Corinthians 2:16, Psalm 119:130, Isaiah 48:17, Proverbs 13:4, Isaiah 40:31, Luke 2:52, Joshua 1:8

Prayer for Parents

Father, I lift my parents before You today. Thank You for their lives and for Your faithfulness toward them. Strengthen them, sustain them, and let Your hand continually guide their steps.

Bless them with health, strength, and peace. Renew their bodies, refresh their minds, and fill their hearts with joy. Let their days be marked by stability, rest, and Your presence.

Provide for every need in their lives. Surround them with Your protection, preserve them wherever they go, and keep them safe under Your care.

Thank You that my parents are loved, honored, and blessed by You. May they walk in wisdom, experience Your goodness, and enjoy the peace and favor that come from Your hand.

In Jesus' name, Amen.

Scripture References: Proverbs 3:2, 3 John 1:2, Proverbs 2:6, Philippians 4:7, Exodus 20:12, Philippians 4:19, Psalm 121:7-8, Nehemiah 8:10, Psalm 16:11

Praying for a Future Wife

Father, I place my desire for a wife before You. You know my life, my future, and the desires of my heart. I trust You to lead me according to Your perfect wisdom and timing.

Prepare the woman You have for me and prepare me to be the husband You have called me to be. Develop within us faith, character, wisdom, humility, and a deep love for You.

Guide our steps and order our paths. Let us recognize one another at the right time and bring us together according to Your plan. Fill my heart with peace, patience, and confidence as I trust in You.

Thank You that Your plans are good. Let our future relationship and marriage be built on love, faithfulness, unity, and a shared commitment to follow You and honor You in all things.

In Jesus' name, Amen.

Scripture References: Genesis 2:18, Proverbs 18:22, Psalm 37:4, Proverbs 3:5-6, Ecclesiastes 3:11, Philippians 4:7, Colossians 3:14, Ephesians 5:25, Jeremiah 29:11

Prayer For A Future Husband

Father, I place my desire for a husband before You. You know my life, my future, and the desires of my heart. I trust You to lead me according to Your perfect wisdom and timing.

Prepare the man You have for me and prepare me to be the wife You have called me to be. Develop within us faith, character, wisdom, humility, and a deep love for You.

Guide our steps and order our paths. Let us recognize one another at the right time and bring us together according to Your plan. Fill my heart with peace, patience, and confidence as I trust in You.

Thank You that Your plans are good. Let our future relationship and marriage be built on love, faithfulness, unity, and a shared commitment to follow You and honor You in all things.

In Jesus' name, Amen.

Scripture References: Genesis 2:18, Psalm 37:4, Proverbs 3:5-6, Ecclesiastes 3:11, Philippians 4:7, Colossians 3:14, Ephesians 5:22-25, Jeremiah 29:11

Godly Relationships and Friendships

Father, thank You for the people You have placed in my life. I am surrounded by relationships that strengthen my faith, encourage my growth, and help me walk in the direction You have called me to go.

Thank you for surrounding me with wise, faithful, and trustworthy people. The relationships in my life sharpen my character, strengthen my decisions, and inspire me to live with purpose and maturity.

My relationships are marked by love, encouragement, loyalty, and peace. The people around me bring wisdom, strength, and support, and together we grow in faith and truth.

Thank You for the friendships, partnerships, and connections You have given me. The people You place in my life are a blessing, and every relationship carries purpose, growth, strength, and encouragement.

In Jesus name, Amen.

Scripture References: Proverbs 13:20, Proverbs 27:17, Proverbs 17:17, 2 Corinthians 6:14, Ephesians 4:15, Romans 12:18, 1 Corinthians 15:33, John 13:34, Ecclesiastes 4:9-10

PRAYERS FOR HEALING

Healing

Father, thank You that Jesus paid the price for my healing. By His stripes I am healed. Your healing power is at work in my body, bringing restoration, strength, and wholeness to every area of my life.

Your Word is life to me and health to all my flesh. Every cell, every organ, and every system in my body comes into alignment with Your design. Strength replaces weakness, and healing replaces sickness.

You are the Lord who heals me. Your life flows through me, renewing what has been damaged, restoring what has been lost, and strengthening what has grown weak. My body responds to Your healing power.

I will live and not die and will declare the works of the Lord. Each day I grow stronger, healthier, and more whole. Thank You for healing, restoration, and life working in me.

In Jesus' name, Amen.

Scripture References: Isaiah 53:5, 1 Peter 2:24, Proverbs 4:20-22, Psalm 103:3, Psalm 107:20, Exodus 15:26, 2 Corinthians 4:16, Psalm 118:17

Recovery from Sickness

Father, You are my healer and my strength. I place my body, my health, and every area of my life into Your hands. Thank You that Your healing power is at work within me.

Healing flows through my body. Strength rises within me. What is weak is strengthened, what is damaged is restored, and what is out of order is brought into alignment. Life and health are being established in me.

Your peace fills my heart and mind. I rest securely in Your care, knowing that You sustain me, uphold me, and walk with me through every stage of recovery.

Thank You for renewing my strength day by day. My body is responding to healing, my spirit is strong, and restoration is taking place. I receive Your healing, Your strength, and Your peace.

In Jesus' name, Amen.

Scripture References: Jeremiah 30:17, Isaiah 40:31, Philippians 4:7, Proverbs 4:20-22, James 1:5, Psalm 103:2-3, Psalm 41:3, Exodus 15:26, 3 John 2, Jeremiah 17:14

Healing For Others

Father, I lift up _________________ before You today and speak healing over their body. By the stripes of Jesus, healing belongs to them. Let Your healing power flow through every part of their body, bringing restoration, strength, and wholeness.

You are the Lord who heals. Let life flow into every cell, every organ, and every system. Restore what has been affected, strengthen what has grown weak, and bring their body into alignment with Your design.

Fill them with Your peace and strength. Remove fear and discouragement, and let confidence and hope rise within them. Sustain them and carry them through every stage of recovery.

I declare that they will live and not die and will declare the works of the Lord. Healing is at work, restoration is taking place, and Your hand is upon them.

In Jesus' name, Amen.

Scripture References: Isaiah 53:5, Exodus 15:26, Psalm 107:20, Jeremiah 30:17, Isaiah 41:10, Philippians 4:7, Psalm 118:17, Psalm 103:2-3, 3 John 2

Prayer Before Surgery

Father, I place _____________ into Your hands as they prepare for surgery. Thank You that Your peace, protection, and presence surround them completely. They are safely held in Your care.

Remove fear and anxiety, and fill their heart with peace, confidence, and rest. Let them know that You are with them every step of the way.

Guide every doctor, surgeon, nurse, and member of the medical team. Give them wisdom, skill, precision, and understanding as they care for _____________.

Let this procedure go smoothly and successfully. Protect their body, strengthen them through every moment, and bring a full recovery. Let healing, restoration, and renewed strength flow into every part of their body.

Thank You for watching over them and sustaining them. Your hand is upon them, Your peace surrounds them, and Your healing power is at work within them.

In Jesus' name, Amen.

Scripture References: Isaiah 41:10, Philippians 4:6-7, James 1:5, Psalm 121:7-8, Jeremiah 30:17, Exodus 15:26, Psalm 46:1, Psalm 91:11, Proverbs 3:5-6, Psalm 28:7

Prayer someone with ADHD

Father, I lift _________________ before You today. Thank You for creating them with purpose, value, and unique gifts that reflect Your design.

Thank You for giving them a spirit of power, love, and a sound mind. Let Your peace fill their heart and mind. Bring clarity, focus, understanding, and confidence into every area of their life.

Strengthen them in their daily responsibilities. Help them to stay focused, and accomplish what is before them. Let wisdom, discipline, and consistency continue developing within them through Your grace.

Thank You that their life has purpose and meaning. The gifts, abilities, and potential You have placed within them are growing and flourishing. Your hand is upon them, Your peace guards them, and Your wisdom leads them each day.

In Jesus name, Amen.

Scripture References: Psalm 139:14, 2 Timothy 1:7, Colossians 3:15, Isaiah 26:3, James 1:5, Romans 12:2, Philippians 4:7, Ephesians 2:10

Prayer Against Dementia

Father, I lift my parent before You today and thank You that You are the Lord who heals. Your healing power is at work in their body, mind, and spirit.

I speak life, healing, and restoration over their mind. They have the mind of Christ. Let clarity, understanding, memory, and soundness increase. Strengthen every part of the brain and nervous system, and let healing flow through every area that has been affected.

Confusion, forgetfulness, and mental decline do not have the final word. Your Word brings life and health. Renew their mind, restore what has been lost, and strengthen their ability to think, remember, communicate, and function with clarity and peace.

Thank You that Your hand is upon them. Fill them with peace, strength, and hope. Their life is held in Your hands, and Your healing power is working within them.

In Jesus' name, Amen.

Scripture References: 1 Corinthians 2:16, Jeremiah 30:17, Isaiah 53:5, Proverbs 4:20-22, Psalm 103:2-3, Romans 12:2, 3 John 2, Exodus 15:26, Jeremiah 17:14, Mark 9:23

PRAYERS FOR PROVISION AND FINANCES

Finances

Father, thank You for being my source and my provider. I trust You to continue providing for every need in my life. I am blessed by You. Your favor rests upon my life, and You bless the work of my hands.

Increase is coming into my life through Your provision and Your favor. You open doors of opportunity, create new possibilities, and bring the right people and resources into my path. What You place in my hands grows and produces fruit.

I walk in wisdom, diligence, generosity, and faithful stewardship. My finances are established in order, peace, and blessing. I have more than enough for my family, for every good work, and to be a blessing to others.

You are my Shepherd, and I lack no good thing. My needs are supplied, my future is secure, and my confidence remains in You. Thank You for Your provision, Your faithfulness, and Your abundant goodness in my life.

In Jesus name, Amen.

Scripture References: James 1:17, Philippians 4:19, Proverbs 3:9-10, Luke 6:38, Malachi 3:10-11, 2 Corinthians 9:6, 2 Corinthians 9:10, 2 Corinthians 9:8, Psalm 35:27, Psalm 23:1

Provision

Father, thank You for Your faithful provision in my life. Every good thing I have comes from Your hand. You have sustained me, cared for me, and provided for me through every season, and my heart is filled with gratitude.

Thank You that You are my Shepherd and I lack no good thing. You have met my needs, opened doors, and made a way for me time and time again. Your faithfulness has never failed me.

Thank You for the work of my hands, for opportunities, for provision, and for the many blessings You have poured into my life. You have been my source, my strength, and my provider, and I acknowledge that all I have comes from You.

My heart is grateful, my soul is at peace, and my trust remains in You. Thank You for Your goodness, Your mercy, and Your constant care. I will remember Your faithfulness and give You praise in every season.

In Jesus' name, Amen.

Scripture References: Philippians 4:19, Matthew 6:8, Psalm 145:16, Matthew 6:33, Matthew 6:11, Psalm 23:1-3, James 1:17, Psalm 103:2, Psalm 90:17, Psalm 23:6

Giving

Father, thank You for being my source and my provider. Every good thing in my life comes from Your hand, and I trust You completely with my finances and with all that You have entrusted to me.

I honor You with my tithes and offerings. I give with a willing, grateful, and joyful heart, knowing that You are faithful in every season. My trust is not in money or possessions, but in You alone. Your Word says, "Give, and it shall be given unto you; good measure, pressed down, shaken together, and running over." Thank You that as I give, You cause provision and blessing to flow according to Your promise.

As I obey Your Word, open the windows of heaven over my life and pour out blessing according to Your promise. Rebuke the devourer, protect what You have entrusted to me, and let Your favor rest upon the work of my hands. Thank You for provision, increase, and abundance. You supply every need according to Your riches in glory.

In Jesus' name, Amen.

Scripture References: Malachi 3:10-11, Proverbs 3:9-10, Philippians 4:19, Luke 6:38, 2 Corinthians 9:6-8, Deuteronomy 8:18, Psalm 23:1, Matthew 6:33, James 1:17

Prosperity

Father, thank You that You are my provider and the source of every good thing in my life. Your blessing is upon me, and Your favor surrounds me.

Increase is coming my way. Doors are opening for me through Your power and according to Your purpose. Opportunities are being placed before me, and You are leading me into the plans You have prepared for my life.

Provision flows into my life according to Your will. Every need is supplied, every step is directed, and every season is covered by Your faithfulness.

I am blessed to be a blessing. Generosity flows through my life, and the resources You place in my hands are used for Your purposes and Your glory.

My life is fruitful, productive, and established by You. Increase, opportunity, provision, and favor are at work in my life because Your hand is upon me.

In Jesus name, Amen.

Scripture References: Deuteronomy 8:18, Deuteronomy 28:8, 11, Psalm 1:3, Psalm 34:10, Malachi 3:10, Matthew 6:3-4, Matthew 6:19-21, Luke 6:38, Acts 10:5, Romans 13:8, 2 Corinthians 9:6-7, Philippians 4:19, 3 John 2

My Bills

Father, You are my provider, and You faithfully supply every need according to Your riches in glory through Christ Jesus. I place every bill, every financial responsibility, and every concern into Your hands.

Thank You that there is provision for every need. You give me wisdom, favor, opportunity, and the ability to prosper. My finances are guided by Your hand and established in Your peace.

I thank You that my bills are paid, my needs are met, and my household is provided for. You bless the work of my hands and bring increase according to Your purpose and timing.

Peace fills my heart as I trust in You. Financial pressure does not control me because You are my source. Your faithfulness sustains me, and Your provision is at work in every area of my life.

In Jesus' name, Amen.

Scripture References: Philippians 4:19, Deuteronomy 28:12, Psalm 90:17, Proverbs 3:9-10, Matthew 6:31-33, Psalm 23:1, Proverbs 24:3-4, Psalm 23:6

Stewardship

Father, thank You that everything I have comes from You. My time, resources, abilities, opportunities, and possessions belong to You, and I desire to steward them faithfully.

Give me wisdom in every decision and discipline in every responsibility. Let integrity guide my choices and excellence mark the work of my hands. Teach me to manage well what You have entrusted to me.

I am faithful with what You have placed in my care. I do not waste opportunities, resources, or gifts. I use them with purpose, gratitude, and wisdom for Your glory.

Thank You for establishing the work of my hands. What You have entrusted to me grows, prospers, and produces fruit. My life is marked by faithfulness, stewardship, and obedience.

In Jesus' name, Amen.

Scripture References: Psalm 24:1, Luke 16:10, James 1:5, Proverbs 11:3, Colossians 3:23, 2 Corinthians 9:7, Proverbs 21:5, Psalm 90:17, James 1:17, Matthew 25:21

Debt

Father, thank You for being my provider and my source. Give me wisdom to manage my finances well and to be a faithful steward of everything You have entrusted to me. Teach me to live within my means, make wise decisions, and honor You with what I have.

Help me walk in discipline and self-control. Strengthen me to resist unnecessary spending, impulsive purchases, and financial habits that do not serve Your purpose for my life. Let wisdom guide my choices and healthy budgeting become part of my daily life.

Thank You for leading me into greater financial freedom. Give me knowledge, understanding, and a clear plan to eliminate debt, build stability, and handle money with confidence and peace. Let diligence, patience, and consistency produce lasting results.

I trust You to supply all my needs according to Your riches in glory through Christ Jesus.

In Jesus' name, Amen.

Scripture References: Philippians 4:19, Proverbs 3:9-10, Proverbs 21:5, Romans 13:8, Luke 14:28, Proverbs 22:7, Matthew 6:31-33, 2 Corinthians 9:8, Psalm 37:25, Deuteronomy 8:18, James 1:5

My Business

Father, I place my business into Your hands. Thank You for the opportunity, the resources, and the abilities You have entrusted to me. Establish the work of my hands and bless what You have called me to build.

Give me wisdom, strategy, discernment, and clear direction in every decision. Lead me to the right opportunities, the right connections, and the right paths for growth. Let favor surround my business and open doors that no one can shut.

Help me honor You through this business. Let it be a tool to support Your kingdom, bless others, and advance the work You have called me to do. Teach me to steward success with humility, generosity, and faithfulness. May what You place in my hands become a blessing to many.

Thank You for Your blessing upon my business. May it grow, prosper, and produce lasting fruit. Let integrity, excellence, and generosity mark everything I do, and may all the glory belong to You.

In Jesus' name, Amen.

Scripture References: Psalm 90:17, Deuteronomy 8:18, Proverbs 3:9-10, Proverbs 11:25, Philippians 4:19, Proverbs 10:22, Matthew 6:33, 2 Corinthians 9:8, Colossians 3:23-24, 1 Corinthians 10:31

Jobs and Work

Father, I place my work into Your hands. Thank You for providing employment and for giving me the ability to work, provide for my family, and be a blessing to others. Help me to work as unto You, with excellence, integrity, and faithfulness in all that I do.

Give me wisdom, favor, and diligence in my workplace. Let my attitude, character, and work reflect Your goodness.

Bless the work of my hands and increase my ability to prosper according to Your purpose. May my employment provide not only for my needs but also give me the opportunity to support Your kingdom through faithful giving, generosity, and obedience. Let me be a channel through which Your blessings flow to others.

Thank You for Your provision and faithfulness. May everything I do bring glory to You, and may my life be marked by stewardship, generosity, and a desire to advance Your kingdom on the earth.

In Jesus' name, Amen.

Scripture References: Colossians 3:23-24, Deuteronomy 8:18, Philippians 4:19, Proverbs 3:9-10, 2 Corinthians 9:8, Malachi 3:10, Psalm 90:17, Matthew 6:33, 1 Corinthians 10:31, Acts 20:35

PRAYERS FOR RESTORATION

Freedom

Father, thank You that true freedom is found in Jesus Christ. Through Him, freedom is established in every part of my life. Whom the Son sets free is free indeed, and I walk in that freedom today. I am free in Christ. My life is no longer defined by my past but by the new life You have given me.

Your grace is at work within me, and Your truth is shaping my life each day. My mind is being renewed, my heart is being restored, and my life is being transformed by the power of The Holy Spirit. Strongholds are torn down, truth is established, and freedom grows within me. Your Word fills my mind with clarity, wisdom, and understanding. I walk in the liberty Christ has given me, and Your presence surrounds my life.

I walk in victory, restoration, and wholeness. Your hand is upon me, and Your power is actively working within me. My future is filled with hope, purpose, and the goodness of God.

In Jesus name, Amen.

Scripture References: John 8:36, Romans 8:1-2, 2 Corinthians 10:4-5, Galatians 5:1, 2 Corinthians 3:17, Romans 12:2, Joel 2:25

Shame

Father, thank You that through Jesus Christ I have been forgiven, cleansed, and made new. I do not stand before You in my own righteousness, but in the righteousness of Christ.

I am the righteousness of God in Christ Jesus. I do not walk in shame, guilt, or condemnation. I will not hide from You in shame because You have forgiven me, accepted me, and welcomed me into Your presence through Your grace.

My sins have been washed away, my past has been redeemed, and my identity is established in You. I am chosen, loved, accepted, and secure. What Jesus accomplished for me is greater than any failure, mistake, or weakness from my past.

Thank You that I can come boldly before Your throne of grace. I walk in freedom, confidence, peace, and righteousness through Jesus Christ. My life is established in Your love, and my future is filled with hope.

In Jesus' name, Amen.

Scripture References: 2 Corinthians 5:21, Romans 8:1, 1 John 1:9, Hebrews 4:16, Ephesians 1:4-7, John 8:36, Romans 5:17, Titus 3:5-7, Hebrews 10:22, Psalm 103:12

Healing From Trauma

Father, thank You for being near to me and surrounding me with Your peace, comfort, and love. You see every wounded place within my heart, and nothing is hidden from Your care.

Thank You for healing the brokenhearted and restoring what has been hurt. Bring healing to every painful memory, every deep wound, and every area affected by trauma. Restore my soul and strengthen my spirit.

Your perfect love drives out fear. Fill me with peace, security, and confidence. My mind is steady, my heart is at rest, and Your presence brings strength and healing each day.

Thank You that You are making all things new. Healing, restoration, and wholeness are growing within me. Your peace guards my heart and mind, and my life is being restored by Your grace.

In Jesus' name, Amen.

Scripture References: Psalm 34:18, Psalm 147:3, Psalm 23:3, 1 John 4:18, 2 Timothy 1:7, 2 Corinthians 5:17, Philippians 4:7, Genesis 50:20, Isaiah 61:1-3

Wounds From The Past

Father, thank You for bringing healing to every wound from my past. I place every hurt, disappointment, failure, painful memory, and broken place into Your hands.

Thank You that You are healing what has been wounded and restoring what has been broken. I am not defined by what happened to me. My identity, value, and purpose are found in You and in who You created me to be.

Your peace guards my heart and mind through Christ Jesus. My heart is being renewed, my emotions are being healed, and my life is being established in freedom, wholeness, and hope.

Thank You that I walk in healing, restoration, and new life through Jesus Christ. My past no longer controls me, my heart is becoming whole, and my future is filled with hope because Your hand is upon my life.

In Jesus' name, Amen.

Scripture References: Psalm 147:3, Colossians 3:13, Isaiah 43:18-19, Proverbs 4:23, Ephesians 4:31-32, 1 Peter 4:8, Romans 8:1, Philippians 4:7, 2 Corinthians 5:17, John 8:36

Deliverance

Father, thank You for being my deliverer, my protector, and my strong refuge. In every season of life, You preserve me, strengthen me, and lead me into freedom. My confidence rests in You because You are faithful, powerful, and always near.

Thank You for bringing freedom and peace into my life through Jesus Christ. Your power continues to work within me, bringing healing, restoration, and renewal. Your truth breaks every barrier, and I walk fully in the life You have called me to live.

Today, I walk in victory, peace, freedom, and restoration through Jesus Christ. Your hand is upon my life, and Your work within me continues to bring wholeness, healing, and growth.

Thank You for surrounding me with Your protection and covering me with Your grace. Your hand is upon my life, and Your light continually shines into every area of my heart and mind.

In Jesus name, Amen.

Scripture References: Psalm 18:2, Psalm 34:4, Colossians 1:13, 2 Corinthians 10:4, Psalm 18:19, John 8:36, Romans 12:2, James 4:7, Isaiah 61:1, Joel 2:25

Freedom from Abandonment

Father, thank You that You are always with me. Your presence surrounds me, strengthens me, and brings peace to my heart. I am never alone because You remain near to me in every season of life.

I belong to You. My life is known, loved, and cared for by You. Your hand is upon me, guiding my steps and establishing my path according to Your purpose.

You are my refuge, my Shepherd, and my safe place. I rest securely in Your love and trust completely in Your faithfulness. Your presence fills me with peace, strength, and confidence.

I declare that I am secure in Christ. I am loved, accepted, protected, and sustained by the Lord. My heart is steady, my life is established, and I remain firmly rooted in His presence.

In Jesus name, Amen.

Scripture References: Hebrews 13:5, Psalm 27:10, Psalm 91:1, Isaiah 43:1, Psalm 34:18, Psalm 8:4, Psalm 23:1, Lamentations 3:22-23

Overcome Rejection

Father, I come before You today and thank You that my identity is found in Jesus Christ. I am accepted in the Beloved, chosen by You, and loved by You. In the name of Jesus, I reject every lie of rejection, unworthiness, abandonment, and inadequacy.

I receive what Your Word says about me. I am loved, accepted, valued, and known by You. My life is established in Your truth and not in the opinions, actions, or decisions of others. Thank You for healing every wounded place in my heart. Your love reaches deeply into every area that has been affected by rejection and fills it with peace, security, and wholeness.

Your acceptance is greater than every hurt I have experienced. I declare that I belong to You. I am chosen, holy, and dearly loved. My identity is rooted in Christ, and my confidence comes from who You say I am. I am fearfully and wonderfully made, created with purpose, value, and meaning.

In Jesus name, Amen.

Scripture References: Psalm 27:10, Colossians 3:12, Ephesians 1:6, Isaiah 43:1, Psalm 147:3, Isaiah 41:10, Psalm 139:14, Ephesians 3:17-18, Romans 8:15-16, 1 John 3:1

Overcoming Failure

Father, thank You that my life is not defined by my failures, mistakes, or past decisions. Through Jesus Christ, I am forgiven, redeemed, and made new. There is no condemnation over my life, and Your grace is greater than every failure I have experienced.

Thank You that when I fall, I rise again. You strengthen me, teach me, and use every season to build wisdom, character, and deeper trust in You. What the enemy meant for harm, You are working together for good according to Your purpose.

I refuse to live in regret, shame, or discouragement. I let go of what is behind and move forward into what You have prepared for me. My steps are ordered by You, and Your purpose for my life remains secure.

Thank You that Your grace is sufficient for me. I rise today with renewed faith, confidence, and hope. I am more than a conqueror through Christ, and the best chapters of my life are still ahead of me.

In Jesus' name, Amen.

Scripture References: Proverbs 24:16, Romans 8:1, Romans 8:28, Philippians 1:6, Philippians 3:13-14, 2 Corinthians 12:9, Romans 8:37, Psalm 37:23-24, Joel 2:25, 2 Corinthians 5:17

Breaking Cycles and Patterns

Father, thank You that through Jesus Christ I am a new creation. Your power is at work within me, bringing freedom, healing, and transformation. My life is not controlled by old patterns, past failures, or unhealthy cycles. I belong to You.

By the power of the Holy Spirit, every destructive pattern and stronghold is being broken. My mind is being renewed, my desires are changing, and my thoughts are coming into alignment with Your truth.

Thank You that generational cycles are replaced with righteousness, wisdom, peace, faith, and spiritual freedom. I am building a new legacy through Christ. My family and future are being shaped by Your truth, Your grace, and Your promises.

What was broken is being restored, what was wounded is being healed, and what was bound is being set free.

In Jesus' name, Amen.

Scripture References: 2 Corinthians 10:4-5, Romans 12:2, John 8:36, Galatians 5:1, Colossians 1:13, 2 Timothy 1:7, Ezekiel 36:26, Romans 6:4, Isaiah 43:18-19, Joel 2:25, 2 Corinthians 5:17

Addiction

Father, thank You that through Jesus Christ I am free. Sin does not have dominion over me, and I am not mastered by any addiction, habit, or stronghold. Whom the Son sets free is free indeed, and I walk in that freedom today.

In the name of Jesus, I break every addiction and every desire that seeks to control my life. Your Spirit is at work within me, producing self-control, strength, and discipline. My mind is being renewed, and my desires are coming into alignment with Your truth.

Every chain is broken. Every stronghold is torn down. I lay aside every weight and move forward in freedom, victory, and purpose. I am strong in the Lord, and Your grace empowers me to overcome.

Thank You that I am a new creation in Christ. Freedom is established in my life, victory is active within me, and I walk daily in the power of Your Spirit.

In Jesus' name, Amen.

Scripture References: Romans 6:14, John 8:36, 2 Corinthians 3:17, 1 Corinthians 6:12, 2 Corinthians 5:17, Romans 8:2, Hebrews 12:1, Galatians 5:22-23, Romans 12:2, Ephesians 6:10

Hatred and Resentment

Father, cleanse my heart from hatred, bitterness, anger, and resentment. Fill me with Your love, Your peace, Your mercy, and Your compassion.

Teach me to love others the way You have loved me. Let grace shape my thoughts, my words, and my actions. Give me patience, kindness, humility, and self-control in every relationship.

I forgive those who have hurt, rejected, misunderstood, or wronged me. I release every offense into Your hands and allow peace and healing to grow within my heart.

Thank You for guarding my heart and renewing my mind. Let compassion, understanding, wisdom, and peace replace judgment, division, and hostility.

I overcome evil with good and walk in love because You are love.

In Jesus' name, Amen.

Scripture References: 1 John 4:20, Ephesians 4:31-32, Colossians 3:13-14, Matthew 5:44, Romans 12:17-21, Galatians 5:22-23, Hebrews 12:15, Proverbs 10:12, 1 Corinthians 13:4-7, 1 John 4:8

Jealousy, Envy, and Comparison

Father, thank You that my identity and worth are found in You. I am secure in Your love, and I trust the purpose and calling You have placed on my life.

Fill my heart with contentment and gratitude. Thank You for Your faithfulness and for the blessings You have given me. My confidence rests in You and not in comparison with others.

I rejoice in the victories and blessings of those around me. Let love, kindness, and encouragement fill my heart as I celebrate what You are doing in their lives.

My eyes remain fixed on You. I am free from jealousy, envy, and comparison. I walk in peace, contentment, and joy, trusting Your timing and Your plan for my life.

In Jesus' name, Amen.

Scripture References: Galatians 6:4, James 3:16, Romans 12:15, Philippians 4:11, Proverbs 14:30, 1

Corinthians 13:4, Colossians 3:15, Psalm 16:5-6, Ephesians 2:10, Hebrews 12:2

Freedom From Anger

Father, thank You for the peace that comes from Your presence and fills my heart each day. Your peace rules within me and steadies my thoughts, emotions, and responses. Father, help me to be quick to listen, patient in understanding, and wise in the way I respond. Let my words be guided by gentleness, self-control, and wisdom. Help me to speak words that bring peace, encouragement, and life.

Your Spirit is producing patience, kindness, peace, and self-control within me. My emotions are steady, my heart is at rest, and my responses reflect the character of Christ. I release offense quickly and walk in forgiveness, grace, and love. My heart remains free, and Your peace continues growing stronger within me each day.

Thank You for strengthening me inwardly by Your Spirit. I walk in peace and reflect Your gentleness in every situation. My life is established in maturity, self-control, and the peace of God.

In Jesus name, Amen.

Scripture References: Colossians 3:15, James 1:19, Proverbs 15:1, Ephesians 4:31, Galatians 5:22-23, Ephesians 4:26-27, Isaiah 26:3, Ephesians 5:2, Ephesians 3:16

Grief

Father, I lift ______________ before You during this time of grief and loss. Surround them with Your presence, Your comfort, and Your peace. Draw near to them and hold them steady through each day.

Thank You that You are close to the brokenhearted and faithful to comfort those who mourn. Strengthen them when they feel weak, carry them when they feel overwhelmed, and fill their heart with Your peace.

Let loving memories bring comfort and gratitude. Surround them with family, friends, and caring people who will encourage, support, and pray for them during this season.

Thank You that Your love never fails and Your presence never leaves. Bring healing to every hurting heart and let hope, peace, and strength rise in the days ahead.

In Jesus' name, Amen.

Scripture References: Psalm 34:18, Matthew 5:4, Psalm 147:3, Isaiah 41:10, John 14:27, Romans 15:13, 2 Corinthians 1:3-4, Psalm 46:1.

PRAYER FOR PROTECTION AND PEACE

God's Protection

Father, You are my defender, my strength, and my deliverer. Every enemy that rises against me is defeated. Today, I walk forward in peace, confidence, and victory knowing Your hand is upon my life.

Strengthen me and lead me in every area of my life. Help me stand firm in faith and remain steady as I place my trust in you. Let my mind stay clear, alert, and focused on what is right and pleasing to You.

Today, I put on the full armor that You have given me and I stand secure in Your truth and righteousness. The weapons You have given me are powerful through You, bringing breakthrough, strength, and victory into every area of my life.

I hold on to the calling and purpose You have placed in me. Through Christ, I am more than a conqueror, and I walk in confidence, peace, and strength each day.

In Jesus name, Amen.

Scripture References: Deuteronomy 28:7, Psalm 35:1-3, Romans 8:37, 2 Corinthians 10:3-4, Ephesians 6:11, 1 Timothy 6:12, 1 Peter 5:8

Protection

Father, You are my refuge, my fortress, and my strong tower. I will not fear because You are with me. I rest confidently in Your protection, knowing that my life is held firmly in Your hands.

I dwell in the secret place of the Most High and remain under the shadow of the Almighty. You surround me with Your favor, cover me with Your presence, and preserve me from every danger. You are my hiding place, my defender, and my shield.

No evil will overpower me, and no weapon formed against me will prosper. You command Your angels concerning me to guard me in all my ways. Every plan of the enemy is exposed and defeated. I am protected, preserved, and kept by the power of God.

I walk in faith, rest in safety, and live under Your divine protection. Victory surrounds me because You are my refuge and my fortress.

In Jesus' name, Amen.

Scripture References: Deuteronomy 33:27, Job 11:18-19, Psalm 9:9, Psalm 32:7, Psalm 52:8-9, Psalm 91:1-2, Psalm 91:9-11, Proverbs 14:26, Isaiah 54:17, Hebrews 6:18

Anxiety

Father, I come before You today and place every concern, every burden, and every anxious thought into Your hands. Your presence brings peace, comfort, and rest to my heart.

I place my trust fully in You. My mind is fixed on Your faithfulness, my heart is anchored in Your promises, and Your peace fills every area of my life. Your peace guards my heart and mind through Christ Jesus. My thoughts are steady, my heart is calm, and my life is established in Your truth. I rest in the confidence that You are working in every situation.

You have given me power, love, and a sound mind. I walk in peace, clarity, and confidence. Your presence renews my strength, quiets my heart, and fills me with assurance.

You are my refuge, my strength, and my peace. I cast every care upon You and receive Your rest. My life is secure in Your hands, and my heart remains established in Your peace.

In Jesus name, Amen.

Scripture References: 1 Peter 5:7, Philippians 4:6-7, Isaiah 26:3, Psalm 56:3, Isaiah 41:10, Isaiah 30:15, 2 Timothy 1:7, Psalm 55:22, Psalm 46:1

Worry

Father, I bring every concern before You. I cast all my cares on You, because You care for me and sustain me. I do not worry about tomorrow. Each day is held in Your hands, and You provide what is needed.

I seek first Your kingdom, and everything else is added. My focus is on You, and my needs are met. You care for me even more than the birds of the air. I am provided for, covered, and kept.

I am not anxious about anything. In everything, I bring my requests to You, and Your peace fills my heart. Your peace guards my heart and my mind. I am steady, calm, and secure.

My mind is stayed on You, and I am kept in perfect peace. My thoughts are settled and at rest.

You are my shepherd; I do not lack. There is provision, rest, and care in You. I trust You completely. My heart is at peace, and worry has no place in me.

In Jesus' name, Amen.

Scripture References: 1 Peter 5:7, Matthew 6:34, Matthew 6:33, Matthew 6:26, Philippians 4:6-7, Isaiah 26:3, Psalm 23:1

Stress

Father, I bring every burden, every concern, and every care to You today. I place everything into Your hands and trust You with what concerns me.

Your presence fills my heart with peace. As I draw near to You, my mind becomes calm, my heart becomes steady, and my soul finds rest. I am not carrying life's pressures alone because You are with me.

You are my refuge, my strength, and my help. I trust You completely. My life is secure in Your hands, and Your peace guards my heart and mind through Christ Jesus.

I release every burden to You and receive Your peace. My thoughts are fixed on You, my confidence is in You, and my strength is renewed by Your presence. You give me wisdom, clarity, and grace for each day.

Thank You for sustaining me and carrying me forward. I walk in peace, rest, and confidence, knowing that You are faithful, You are near, and You are taking care of me.

In Jesus name, Amen.

Scripture References: 1 Peter 5:7, Matthew 11:28-30, Psalm 46:1-2, Isaiah 26:3, Philippians 4:7, Psalm 62:8, Isaiah 30:15, Psalm 46:10, Isaiah 40:31, Isaiah 41:10

Protection From My Enemies

Father, thank You for being my defender, my refuge, and my shield. You see every situation clearly, and I trust You to protect me, uphold me, and fight on my behalf.

No weapon formed against me will prosper. You surround me with favor as with a shield, and Your angels watch over me. I rest securely under Your protection and care.

I choose to forgive those who have hurt me, opposed me, or spoken against me. I release every offense into Your hands and allow Your peace and grace to fill my heart.

Thank You for turning every situation for good. You are my strong tower, my deliverer, and my source of victory. My life is secure in You, and my confidence remains in Your faithfulness.

In Jesus' name, Amen.

Scripture References: Isaiah 54:17, Psalm 35:1, Psalm 91:1-11, Matthew 6:14-15, Colossians 3:13, Proverbs 18:10, Genesis 50:20, Romans 12:21, Psalm 3:3, Psalm 5:12

Praying for My Enemies

Father, I forgive those who have hurt me and have said all manner of evil against me. I release them into Your hands and choose to walk in forgiveness, grace, and freedom. Thank You for helping me let go of every offense and trust You with every situation.

I place them completely into Your hands. You are the righteous Judge, and I trust Your wisdom, Your justice, and Your mercy in every circumstance.

I bless those who have come against me and pray for them. I release every offense, every hurt, and every disappointment. My heart remains free from bitterness and resentment.

Thank You for being my defender, my refuge, and my shield. You fight my battles. My peace and confidence is found in You, and my life is securely held in Your hands.

In Jesus' name, Amen.

Scripture References: Matthew 5:44, Romans 12:14, Colossians 3:13, James 1:19, Romans 12:17-21, Isaiah 54:17, Psalm 18:2, Ephesians 5:11, Romans 12:18, Psalm 35:1, Proverbs 16:7

SPIRITUAL WARFARE

Spiritual Warfare

In the name of Jesus, I bind every work of the enemy that seeks to oppose Your purposes in my life. I declare that no weapon formed against me shall prosper. Every strategy of the enemy is exposed by Your light and defeated by Your power.

I come against every attack directed toward my mind, my family, my faith, my calling, and my future. I declare that Jesus is Lord, and I walk in the authority and victory He has provided.

Every lie is replaced with truth, and every scheme of the enemy is overcome through the authority of Jesus Christ.

Thank You that You lead me in triumph. I walk in victory, freedom, authority, and purpose. Your hand is upon me, Your angels surround me, and Your Spirit strengthens me each day.

In Jesus name, Amen.

Scripture References: Isaiah 54:17, Matthew 16:19, Luke 10:19, Ephesians 6:10-17, 2 Corinthians 10:4-5, James 4:7, Revelation 12:11, Colossians 2:15, 2 Corinthians 2:14, Psalm 91:11

Binding the Enemy Of My Soul

Father, thank You that through Jesus Christ I stand in victory, freedom, and spiritual authority. I resist the devil, and he flees from me.

In the name of Jesus, I bind every assignment of the enemy sent against my life. I loose the peace of God, the wisdom of God, the protection of God, and the power of the Holy Spirit over my life, my family, and all You have entrusted to me.

No weapon formed against me will prosper. The blood of Jesus covers me, Your angels surround me, and Your truth guards my heart and mind. Every stronghold is broken, every thought is brought into obedience to Christ, and every scheme of the enemy is defeated.

Greater is He who is in me than he who is in the world. I stand firm in faith, clothed in the armor of God, and established in Your peace, Your truth, and Your power.

In Jesus' name, Amen.

Scripture References: Matthew 16:19, Matthew 18:18, James 4:7, Luke 10:19, Isaiah 54:17, 2 Corinthians 10:5, Ephesians 6:11-18, Revelation 12:11, Colossians 1:13, John 8:36, 1 John 4:4, Ephesians 2:6, Romans 8:37

Lust

Father, strengthen me to walk in purity, holiness, and self-control. My body is the temple of the Holy Spirit, and I desire to honor You with my thoughts, my actions, and my choices.

Guard my eyes, my mind, and my heart. Give me wisdom to recognize temptation and the strength to turn away from it quickly. Let Your Word remain alive within me, renewing my mind and guiding my steps.

Thank You that no temptation is greater than Your grace. You always provide a way of escape, and through the power of the Holy Spirit I have the strength to choose what is pure, righteous, and pleasing to You.

Whom the Son sets free is free indeed. I walk in freedom, purity, and victory through Jesus Christ. My heart belongs to You, my mind is being renewed, and my life is being established in holiness and obedience.

In Jesus' name, Amen.

Scripture References: 1 Corinthians 10:13, 2 Timothy 2:22, Galatians 5:16, 1 Corinthians 6:18-20, Job 31:1, Psalm 119:9-11, Romans 12:2, Galatians 5:22-23, John 8:36, Matthew 5:8

A Lying Spirit

Father, let truth rule in my heart, my mind, and my words. Search me, cleanse me, and establish integrity within me. I desire to live honestly before You and before others.

Guard my mouth and guide my speech. Let my words be truthful, trustworthy, and full of grace. Remove every tendency toward exaggeration, deception, half-truths, and falsehood. Let honesty become a way of life for me.

Your Spirit is the Spirit of truth. Renew my mind through Your Word and help me walk in humility, sincerity, and transparency. Let my thoughts, motives, and actions reflect the character of Christ.

Thank You that truth brings freedom. I walk in the light as You are in the light. My life is marked by honesty, integrity, and righteousness, and my heart remains open and clean before You.

In Jesus' name, Amen.

Scripture References: John 8:32, Ephesians 4:25, Proverbs 12:22, Psalm 51:6, Colossians 3:9-10, James 3:17, Psalm 141:3, 1 John 1:7, John 16:13, Philippians 4:8

Demonic Attacks

In the name of Jesus, I bind every demonic attack, every lying spirit, every spirit of fear, oppression, confusion, intimidation, and discouragement that would seek to work against my life, my family, my peace, or my purpose. I declare that every assignment of darkness is broken and rendered powerless through the authority of Jesus Christ.

I loose the peace of God, the wisdom of God, the protection of God, and the power of the Holy Spirit over my life. The blood of Jesus covers me and my household. No weapon formed against me will prosper, and every scheme of the enemy is defeated through Christ.

I put on the whole armor of God and stand firm in faith. Thank You for surrounding me with Your presence, Your angels, and Your protection. Greater is He who is in me than he who is in the world. I walk in freedom, victory, peace, and spiritual authority through Jesus Christ.

In Jesus' name, Amen.

Scripture References: Matthew 16:19, Matthew 18:18, Isaiah 54:17, James 4:7, Luke 10:19, Ephesians 6:11-17, Revelation 12:11, 2 Corinthians 10:4-5, Psalm 91:11, Colossians 1:13, 2 Timothy 1:7, 1 John 4:4, Luke 10:17-19

Nightmares

Father, thank You for Your peace, protection, and presence as I rest tonight. I place myself, my family, and my home into Your hands. I dwell under the shadow of the Almighty, and no fear, darkness, or evil has authority over me because I belong to Jesus Christ.

In the name of Jesus, I take authority over every spirit of fear, anxiety, torment, oppression, and disturbance. I bind every attack against my mind, my sleep, and my peace. Every troubling thought, nightmare, and assignment of the enemy is broken through the authority of Jesus Christ.

I declare that my home is covered by the blood of Jesus. The peace of God fills every room, and the presence of the Holy Spirit rests upon this house. No weapon formed against us will prosper, and no evil will come near our dwelling. Thank You for sweet sleep. My mind is at rest, my heart is at peace, and my body is refreshed. I lie down in peace and sleep in safety because You alone make me dwell securely.

In Jesus' name, Amen.

Scripture References: Psalm 4:8, Psalm 91:1-11, Philippians 4:7, Proverbs 3:24, Isaiah 26:3, 2 Timothy 1:7, Matthew 11:28-29, Isaiah 54:17, Luke 10:19, Revelation 12:11, Psalm 34:7, Psalm 23:3.

PRAYERS FOR CHURCH AND MINISTRY

Church

Father, thank You for my church and for the work You are building through it. Let this house remain firmly established on Jesus Christ, strong in truth, filled with Your presence, and led by Your Spirit.

Fill this church with Your power and peace. Let lives be transformed, hearts restored, and people drawn closer to You through Your Word and the work of the Holy Spirit. Let salvation, healing, freedom, and spiritual growth flourish in this house.

Let unity, love, honor, and encouragement mark this church. Protect us from division, offense, gossip, and strife. Strengthen every relationship and help us walk together in humility, grace, and peace.

Bless our pastors, leaders, and congregation with wisdom, strength, and favor. Provide for every need, expand our influence, and let this church be a light in our community that brings glory to Jesus Christ.

In Jesus' name, Amen.

Scripture References: Matthew 16:18, Colossians 1:18, Acts 2:47, Ephesians 4:3, Hebrews 13:17, Acts 4:30, Philippians 4:19, Matthew 5:16.

Unity for the Church

Father, let unity fill this church. Join our hearts together in love, peace, humility, and truth so that we walk together as one body in Christ. Let the bond of peace and the love of Jesus strengthen every relationship in this house.

In the name of Jesus, we bind every spirit of division, offense, gossip, strife, jealousy, pride, and confusion. Let every scheme of the enemy against this church be stopped and brought to nothing. Expose every hidden agenda, every work of darkness, and everything that seeks to disrupt what You are building. Let those who desire peace, unity, and righteousness be strengthened, and let every divisive influence lose its power and effectiveness.

Protect our pastors, leaders, and congregation. Give us discernment to recognize what is not from You and wisdom to walk in truth. Fill this church with love, unity, healing, and spiritual growth. May Jesus be glorified, lives be transformed in this church.

In Jesus' name, Amen.

Scripture References: Psalm 133:1, Ephesians 4:2-3, John 17:21, Colossians 3:13-14, Ephesians 4:29, Proverbs 6:16-19, Romans 16:17, Titus 3:10, Colossians 3:15, 1 Corinthians 12:12, Acts 2:1, Luke 8:17.

The Persecuted Church Around The World

Father, I lift up my brothers and sisters in Christ who are suffering persecution around the world. Strengthen them with power through Your Spirit. Let them stand bold, unshaken, and unwavering in their faith, no matter what they face.

Protect them, sustain them, and provide for every need. Let fear have no place in their hearts. Fill them with courage, peace, and supernatural strength as they faithfully follow Jesus. Let no attack of the enemy move them from their faith.

May their witness shine brightly in the darkness. Let many come to salvation through their testimony, and let the persecuted church grow stronger, more united, and more powerful through the work of the Holy Spirit.

In Jesus' name, Amen.

Scripture References: Hebrews 13:3, Acts 4:29-31, Isaiah 40:31, Ephesians 3:16, 2 Timothy 1:7, Philippians 4:19, Matthew 5:16.

My Pastors

Father, I lift up my pastors before You. Strengthen them with power through the Holy Spirit. Fill them with wisdom, discernment, courage, and spiritual strength as they faithfully lead and serve Your people.

Protect their minds, hearts, families, health, and ministries. Surround them with Your peace, favor, and protection. Let no weapon formed against them prosper, and let every assignment of the enemy be broken.

Anoint them to preach and teach Your Word with boldness, clarity, truth, and love. Let their lives reflect the character of Christ, and let their ministry bear lasting fruit for Your kingdom.

Refresh and renew them daily. Fill them with joy, endurance, and a fresh passion for Your presence. Bless the work of their hands, strengthen their families, and let Your hand remain upon them in every season.

In Jesus' name, Amen.

Scripture References: James 1:5, Acts 4:29, Psalm 121:7-8, Ephesians 3:16, Isaiah 30:21, Ephesians 6:11, Proverbs 11:3, John 15:16, Nehemiah 8:10, Isaiah 54:17.

Missionaries

Father, I lift up missionaries and those carrying the gospel around the world. Fill them with boldness, wisdom, endurance, and the power of the Holy Spirit. Strengthen them to faithfully proclaim Jesus Christ wherever You send them.

Open doors for the gospel and prepare hearts to receive Your truth. Let lives be transformed, souls be saved, and communities be changed through the power of Your Word.

Protect them physically, spiritually, emotionally, and mentally. Surround them with Your presence, Your peace, and Your angels. Let no weapon formed against them prosper, and keep them safe wherever they go.

Provide abundantly for every need. Supply the finances, resources, partnerships, favor, and support needed to accomplish the work You have called them to do. Refresh them daily, strengthen their families, and let their labor produce lasting fruit for Your kingdom.

In Jesus' name, Amen.

Scripture References: Acts 1:8, Colossians 4:3, Acts 4:29-30, Psalm 121:7-8, Philippians 4:19, Isaiah 40:31, Romans 10:14-15, Matthew 9:37-38, 2 Corinthians 9:8.

PRAYER FOR LEADERS AND THE WORLD

Global Peace

Father, let Your peace spread across the nations of the world. Bring healing where there is suffering, unity where there is division, and reconciliation where there is conflict. Let Your mercy and grace be revealed among the peoples of the earth.

Give wisdom and discernment to leaders and those in authority. Let decisions be guided by justice, humility, compassion, and a desire for peace. Restrain violence, hatred, and corruption, and let what is right prevail.

Protect innocent lives and strengthen those affected by war, persecution, disaster, and unrest. Bring comfort to the hurting, provision to those in need, and hope to those living in fear.

Let the gospel of Jesus Christ continue spreading throughout the earth. Draw hearts to salvation, fill nations with Your peace, and let Your will be done on earth as it is in heaven.

In Jesus' name, Amen.

Scripture References: Matthew 5:9, Psalm 46:9, 1 Timothy 2:1-2, Isaiah 2:4, Philippians 4:7, Micah 6:8, John 14:27, Matthew 6:10.

My Government / President

Father, I lift up the president and all those in authority before You. Give them wisdom, discernment, integrity, and understanding. Let their decisions be guided by truth, justice, and righteousness.

Surround our leaders with wise counsel and people who will speak truth with courage and honesty. Let what is right be upheld, and let wisdom guide the direction of our nation.

Bring peace, protection, stability, and order across this land. Expose corruption, deception, and confusion, and let truth, justice, and righteousness prevail.

As Your people, we pray for our nation and its leaders. Let Your will be done, Your purposes be established, and Your blessing rest upon this country according to Your mercy and grace.

In Jesus' name, Amen.

Scripture References: 1 Timothy 2:1-2, Proverbs 21:1, Daniel 2:21, Proverbs 11:14, Proverbs 29:2, Romans 13:1, 2 Chronicles 7:14.

Our Nation

Father, I lift up my nation before You. Let Your hand rest upon this land and bring wisdom, peace, righteousness, and truth. May Your blessing and favor be upon our country. Guide our leaders with wisdom, discernment, humility, and integrity. Let justice prevail, truth be upheld, and decisions be made for the good of the people. Let righteousness exalt this nation.

Your Word says, "If My people who are called by My name will humble themselves, pray, seek My face, and turn from their wicked ways, then I will hear from heaven, forgive their sin, and heal their land." Lord, I humble myself before You and repnt of my sin. Bring healing, restoration, and spiritual renewal to this nation.

Let the gospel of Jesus Christ spread across this land with power. Bring revival, awakening, and a turning of hearts back to You. May Your will be done, Your truth be established, and Your name be glorified throughout our nation.

In Jesus' name, Amen.

Scripture References: 2 Chronicles 7:14, Psalm 33:12, Proverbs 14:34, 1 Timothy 2:1-2, Micah 6:8, Matthew 5:9, Habakkuk 2:14.

Our Military

Father, I lift up the men and women serving in our military before You. Surround them with Your protection, strength, wisdom, and peace wherever they are stationed. Watch over them, keep them safe, and let Your presence remain with them at all times.

Strengthen them with courage, endurance, discipline, and clarity. Protect them physically, emotionally, mentally, and spiritually. Let no fear, discouragement, or harm overcome them, and give them wisdom in every situation they face.

I also lift up their families at home. Surround them with peace, provision, comfort, and strength. Sustain marriages, protect children, and fill their homes with Your presence while they are separated from their loved ones.

Thank You for those who serve and sacrifice for others. Let Your hand remain upon them and their families. May Your protection, favor, and peace rest upon them, and may they return home safely and strengthened.

In Jesus' name, Amen.

Scripture References: Psalm 91:1-11, Isaiah 41:10, Psalm 121:7-8, Joshua 1:9, Philippians 4:7, 2 Thessalonians 3:3, Deuteronomy 31:6, Psalm 46:1, John 14:27.

About The Author

Tom Flores is the lead pastor of Elevate Life Church in Riverside, California, where he serves alongside his wife, Heather Flores. Pastor Tom has dedicated his life to preaching the Gospel with a strong focus on faith, healing, restoration, and helping people overcome life's struggles through the power of God's Word.

For speaking engagements and additional resources, please visit www.tomflores.com

www.ingramcontent.com/pod-product-compliance
Lightning Source LLC
Chambersburg PA
CBHW061431150726
47987CB00001B/170